POCKET **BIKE** **MAINTENANCE**

The step-by-step guide to bicycle repairs

First published in 2017

10 9 8 7 6 5 4 3 2 1

Copyright © Carlton Books Limited 2017

A CIP catalogue record for this book is available from the British Library

ISBN 978 1 78097 953 3

Printed and bound in China

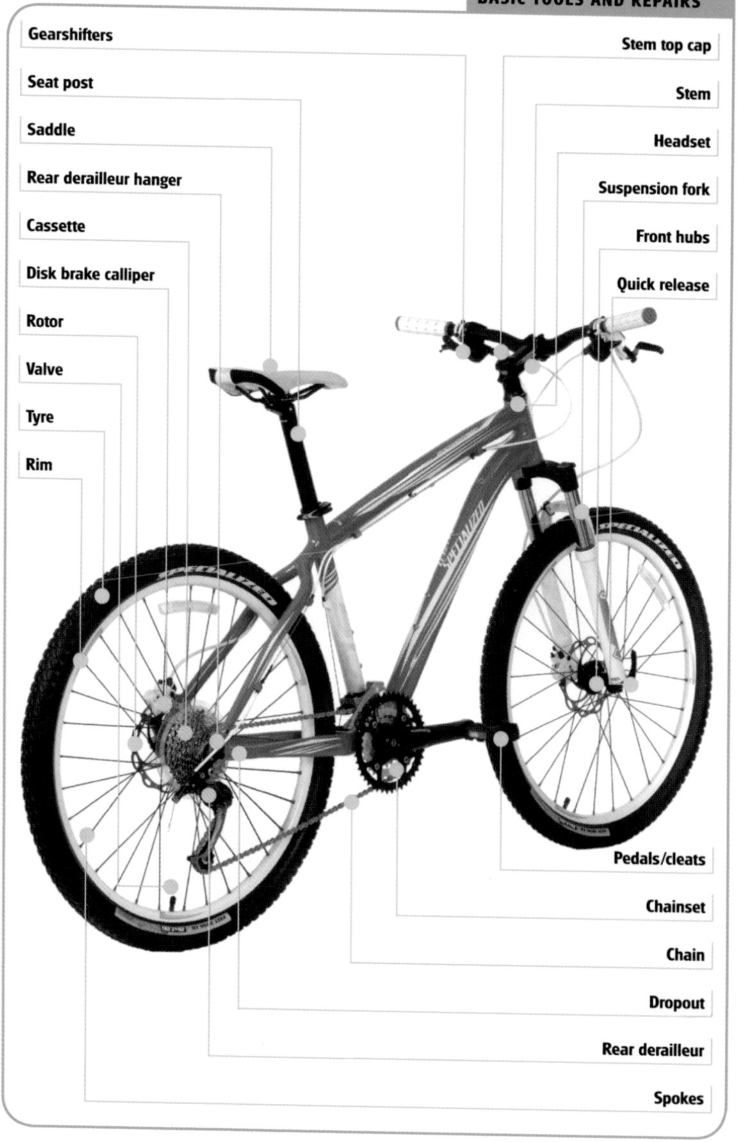

Gearshifters

Seat post

Saddle

Rear derailleur hanger

Cassette

Disk brake calliper

Rotor

Valve

Tyre

Rim

Stem top cap

Stem

Headset

Suspension fork

Front hubs

Quick release

Pedals/cleats

Chainset

Chain

Dropout

Rear derailleur

Spokes

Chain: The chain connects your chainset to your cassette so that when you pedal the back wheel goes around. It needs to be strong so it doesn't snap when you stand on your pedals and stamp up a hill, but it must also be flexible, so that it can shift from side to side across the cassette and chainset. Chain width needs to match your cassette: for example, nine-speed cassettes have narrower, more closely spaced sprockets than older eight-speeds so you need a narrower chain.

Headset: The main bearing at the front of your bike, the headset, connects your forks to your frame. This part is often ignored because it's mostly hidden in the frame. This bearing must be adjusted so it turns smoothly without rattling – any play or binding will affect your bike's handling. There are two types of headset: the newer "Aheadset" type shown here has almost completely superseded the older threaded headset. Regular servicing keeps bearings running smoothly and helps your headset last longer.

Bottom bracket: Bottom brackets are another "out-of-sight, out-of-mind" component. The bottom bracket axle connects your two cranks together through the frame. If worn and loose, the bottom bracket can lead to front gear shifting problems and cause your chain to wear out. Worn bottom brackets can be spotted by checking for side to side play in your cranks. Usually supplied as a sealed unit, this part must be replaced when worn or stiff. This repair needs a couple of specific but inexpensive tools.

Pedals: Introduced from road bikes, clipless pedals have replaced toe clips: a key-shaped cleat on the bottom of your shoe locks into a sprung mechanism on your pedals. The idea of clipless pedals is daunting for the first-timer, but you'll appreciate the extra power once you are used to them. Because your shoe is firmly attached, all your energy throughout the pedal stroke is used. Clean, oiled cleats will release your shoe instantly when you twist your foot. Many riders prefer flat pedals with studs.

Hubs: Well-adjusted hub bearings let wheels spin freely and save you energy. When properly adjusted, your bearings will be tight enough to prevent any side to side play without being so tight they slow you down. Occasional servicing to clean out any grit and dirt that has worked its way in will keep your wheels turning smoothly. Fresh, clean grease helps keep moisture out of your hubs. Jet-washing is tempting after a muddy ride, but will drive water in past your hub seals, flushing out the grease.

Suspension: Suspension makes your ride smoother. Almost all new mountain bikes come with front suspension forks, and full suspension bikes (with front suspension forks and a rear shock unit) get lighter and cheaper every year. Suspension bikes are better because they absorb trail shock and make you faster over uneven ground. The suspension keeps your centre of gravity moving forwards rather than up and down. Front forks and rear shocks need setting up for your weight and riding style.

Tools and equipment

Of course, everyone starts off with very basic equipment. Then gradually, as you get more confident fixing your bike, you find you need various other pieces of gear. Your toolkit grows and grows, until it reaches the happy point where you can tackle complicated tasks without investing in any more tools.

The evolving toolkit

Some tools are universal, like screwdrivers. Others are highly specific and only do one task, or even just one task on one particular make and model of component. When I was 18, I bought a socket to change the oil on my VW Beetle car. I sold the car a couple of years later, but the socket hung out in my toolbox until I didn't notice it any more. One day I cleared out my toolbox and realized I hadn't used it in 15 years – now it makes a nice candlestick on my bathtub. You can always find a new task for old tools so hang on to them.

The tools on the first list are good for a start and should allow you to carry out all the simple repairs you need. As your toolkit grows, a clear distinction will develop between your trail tools and your workshop tools. Trail tools need to be small and light and preferably foldable, so they don't stab you from inside a pocket when you fall off your bike. With workshop tools, the bigger and chunkier the better, first for proper leverage, and second so they last longer without wearing out. Neat and lightweight gadget tools will wear quickly if they get used frequently in the workshop.

Manuals and instructions are tools too

All new bikes and parts come with manuals or instructions. For some reason, it's traditional to throw them away without reading them. I don't know why. Don't do it.

Keep all instructions and manuals together: they're part of your toolkit. It is particularly important to keep the original manual for suspension parts as fitting and setting-up instructions vary between make, model and year.

Once you find yourself using the manuals, feel free to scribble your own notes and diagrams on them as your knowledge grows.

The simple toolkit

When I started working on this section, I wrote and rewrote for the better part of a morning, adding and deleting items I believed were essential until, finally, I was happy with the result.

Then a friend came round, and together we calculated that the total cost of all the tools was more than her bike. I started again. The result is two lists: one of indispensable tools and a second for when you get more confident.

The second list is broken down to match chapters of the book, so you can buy items as you go along. Some tools are bike-specific. Some are obtainable from hardware or tool stores. Good tools last for years and are an investment. Cheap tools let you down when you least need it and can damage the component you're trying to fix. A plastic toolbox costs very little, and both keeps tools together and protects them from damage.

Don't lend your tools to anyone. This sounds harsh, but if you like someone enough to lend them a spanner, fix their bike for them instead. If you don't like them enough to fix their bike, you don't trust them enough to lend them your spanner.

The basic toolkit

The tools on this page are the indispensable ones you'll need to carry out the most basic repairs and maintenance on your bike.

◆ **Allen keys.** The best starter packs are fold-up sets of metric spanners (keys) that include 2, 2.5, 3, 4, 5 and 6mm sizes. You can use the body of the tool as a handle and bear down hard on it without bruising your hand. I'd rather choose a set with a wider range of keys than those you get that also come with screwdrivers, which are intended for trail use. Later, you will want separate Allen keys as they are actually easier to use. Those with a ball at one end allow you to get into awkward spaces.

◆ **A long-handled (about 200mm [8 inch]) 8mm or 10mm Allen key** is essential for most current crank bolts, which attach the pedals to the bottom bracket in the body of the bike. Older crank bolts take a 14mm socket.

◆ **Screwdrivers:** you'll need one flathead and one No.2 Phillips.

◆ **Metric spanners.** The 8, 9, 10, 15 and 17mm sizes are the most useful, but a metric spanner set that's got all the sizes from 8 to 17mm is ideal. The best are combination spanners, with a ring at one end (to grip all round the nut) and an open end at the other (easier to get into awkward spaces).

◆ **A big adjustable spanner,** also called a crescent spanner, with a 200mm-long [8 inch] handle is a good size to start with. The jaws must open to at least 32mm (1¼ inches). Always tighten the jaws firmly onto the flats of the nut before applying pressure to the handle to avoid damaging the nut and the jaws.

◆ **Good quality, bike-specific wirecutters** – not just pliers – can be purchased from your local bike shop. This tool can seem expensive, but both inner cable and outer casing must be cut neatly and cleanly.

◆ **Chain tool.** Again, quality really makes the difference. It's easy to damage an expensive chain with a cheap chain tool.

◆ **Chain-wear measuring tool.** An essential, this tool shows when your chain has stretched enough to damage other parts of the drivetrain.

◆ **A sharp knife with a retractable blade,** so you don't cut yourself digging in your toolbox for a spanner, is useful for cutting open packaging, releasing zipties (cable or electrical ties), etc.

◆ **A pair of pliers.**

◆ **A rubber or plastic mallet.** You can get these from hardware stores. A metal hammer is not a suitable alternative!

◆ **Puncture kit for standard and/or UST tubeless tyres.**

◆ **Track pump.** Frame-clipping pumps are intended for the trail, while a track pump gets plenty of air into the tires without you busting a gut. They're virtually essential for UST tubeless tires. Get one with its own pressure gauge, or buy a separate pressure gauge.

Sling a pen and notebook into your toolbox for making notes and drawing pictures as you take things apart.

It will help you reassemble them later. It's also useful for noting tyre pressures and suspension settings.

The comprehensive toolkit

As you develop a bit of expertise and start to tackle the major jobs, you have to add to your basic toolkit.

Brakes

If you use disc brakes, you need a bleed kit. You can either improvise one from tubes and bottles, or buy a specific one for your brakes. If you haven't bled brakes before, a kit makes it a lot easier. You should be able to tackle everything else with the basic toolkit.

Brake-bleeding kit

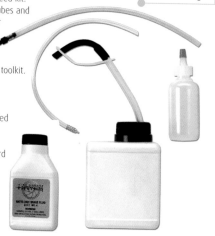

Bottom bracket and headset
Headset spanners

You only need these for older, threaded headsets, which come in three sizes: 32mm (formerly standard), 36mm (called "oversize" but actually standard now) and 40mm (evolution size). Aheadsets are adjusted with Allen keys and don't need a spanner.

Bottom bracket tools

The most common style is the Shimano splined remover. This takes either a large adjustable spanner or a 32mm headset spanner. Remember, the right-hand side of the frame has a reverse thread. Facing the right-hand side of the bike, the right-hand cup is removed clockwise. Facing the left-hand side, the left-hand cup is removed counterclockwise. Splined designs are wider than the older square taper ones; if you have an older version of the tool, the hole in the middle may not be big enough to fit over the splined axle. Sorry, you will just have to buy a new tool.

Headset spanners

Splined removers

Transmission

- **Chain-cleaning box.**
- **Brush for chain cleaning.**
- **Crank extractor(s).** Essential for removing cranks and accessing the bottom bracket. You will need a spanner to drive the inner part of the extractor once the body is firmly screwed into the crank. The cranks are refitted using just the crank bolts – you don't need the extractor for this. There are two types of extractor: one for the newer splined axles, the other for the older square taper axles. An adapter allows you to use a square-type tool with splined axles, but splined tools will not fit square taper axles.

- **Cassette-remover and chain whip.** The cassette-remover fits into the splines at the centre of the cassette. You then need a big adjustable spanner to turn the tool. The chain whip fits around a sprocket and prevents the cassette turning as you undo its lockring. You don't need the chain whip for refitting the lockring; the ratchet in the middle of the cassette stops the cassette turning.
- **For freewheels** – how rear cogs were fitted on your wheel before cassettes were invented – you need the appropriate freewheel tool.

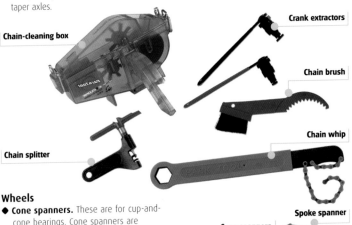

Crank extractors

Chain-cleaning box

Chain brush

Chain whip

Chain splitter

Wheels

- **Cone spanners.** These are for cup-and-cone bearings. Cone spanners are very thin so they can slot onto the narrow flats on the cones. Common sizes are 13, 15 and 17mm, but you'd best take your wheels to the bike shop and check the size before you buy.
- **Spoke spanner,** to fit your spokes. Take your wheels to the bike shop to check the size. Too small won't fit, too big will round off the nipple, which is really annoying.

Spoke spanner

Cone spanners

Suspension
Shock tools

◆ These depend on the make and model of the shock. Check the owner's manual (which you have neatly filed!) for the tool list. If you have lost the manual, most are available on the net.

◆ **Air-sprung forks need a shock pump.** These have narrow barrels and accurate gauges to allow a precise volume of air into your shocks. If you buy a new air fork it may include a shock pump. You can also get tiny trail versions to fit in your pocket when you're out riding.

◆ **A small plastic measuring jug** for shock oil or a **plastic syringe.** They sell these in chemists for measuring out baby medicine.

Suspension pump

Plastic syringe

Suspension fluid

Components
Pedal spanners

All makes of pedals except Time use a 15mm spanner. Pedal spanners are narrower than normal spanners so they can slot in between the pedal and crank, and are longer for extra leverage. Pedals must be fitted snugly or they work loose and rip out the crank threads. Some pedals use an Allen key, accessed from the back of the crank. For these you need a good-quality extra-long (200mm [8 inch]) Allen key or an extender bar.

Pedal spanner

Spare parts box

You need a box of spare parts as well. It's worth keeping bits and pieces in your house so you don't have to rush off in the middle of a job to pick them up.

◆ **Two tubes** the right size, with the correct valve for your wheels.
◆ **Brake blocks or pads.**

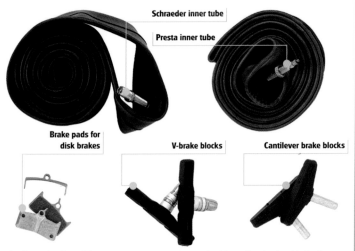

Schraeder inner tube

Presta inner tube

Brake pads for disk brakes

V-brake blocks

Cantilever brake blocks

◆ **A) Two brake cables.**
◆ **B) Two gear cables** and a length of gear outer casing.
◆ **C) Ferrules** (the end caps on casing) and end caps (the end caps on cables).
◆ **D) For Shimano chains:** chain-joining pins.
◆ **E) Zipties** (aka cable or electrical ties). These hold the fabric of the universe together. Before them we had string. Mountain biking couldn't exist until the ziptie was invented. Whoever invented it deserves a major international prize. No toolbox should be without a few of them.
◆ **F) Electrical tape.**

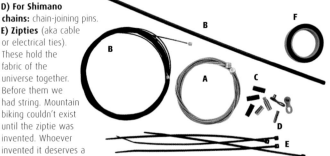

The biscuit box

One of the most irritating parts of bike repair is being thwarted by a simple task because you're missing a simple but very specific part. Bike shop workshops always have racks of plastic drawers full of tiny little parts, many of which are essential for just one job. This is a luxury you're unlikely to have at home.

Your tackle box is essential but, like a good compost heap, it must grow over time and cannot be bought wholesale! Start one now. A tackle box is any container into which you drop odd nuts and bolts left over from other bike repairs. When you shear off an essential bolt just after the stores have closed, your box of bits can save your bacon.

The box should be bike-specific – surplus woodscrews and outdated distributor caps don't count. Useful things include M5 (5mm diameter) bolts in lengths from 10mm to 45mm, crank bolts, Aheadset caps with rude slogans on them, odd washers, valve caps, ball bearings and scraps of chain.

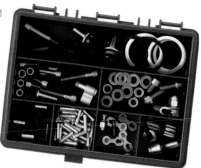

Your workshop

A proper workstand is probably your most expensive investment. Almost all the procedures listed in the main part of this book are easier if the bike is held steady with both wheels off the ground. Working standing up is easier than working crouched on the ground. A workstand also allows you to turn the pedals and wheels and observe everything working.

The next level down from a full workstand is a propstand, which keeps the back wheel off the ground and holds the bike upright.

If you have nothing, then improvise. Avoid turning the bike upside down – bikes don't like it. Instead, find an obedient friend who will hold the bike upright and off the ground at appropriate moments.

You need enough light to see by, especially for close-up jobs such as truing wheels. Most repairs are pretty messy. If you're working indoors, spread an old sheet on the floor before you start to catch things that drop. Ventilation is important. Any time you use solvents or spray, you need enough air circulating to dilute chemical fumes to harmless levels. Anything powerful enough to sweeten your bike will probably damage your body.

The same goes for bodily contact with substances. Consider wearing mechanics' rubber gloves. This saves loads of time cleaning your hands and reduces the quantity of chemicals absorbed through your skin. Lots of jobs involve removing something dirty, then either cleaning it or replacing it, before re-fitting it. You must have clean hands for the last part of the job – there's no point fitting a clean component with dirty hands.

Potions and lotions

A supply of cleaning and lubricating products is essential for routine maintenance. Your bike shop will usually have a choice. Ask for their recommendations, since they'll know what works well for your local environment. As you tackle more advanced jobs, you'll need some more specialized items.

Cleaning products

Always start with the least aggressive cleaning products, then gradually intensify.

◆ **A cleaning fluid**, for example Pedro's Bio Degreaser or Finish Line Bike Wash, both available in the US, or Muc-Off, available in the UK, makes washing quicker. Spray it on and leave it to soak in. In dry, dusty conditions you can wipe it off. Otherwise, rinse with clean water.

◆ **Degreaser**. This is great for cleaning up dirty drivetrains. Spray or paint it onto chain, front rings and cassettes; leave it to soak in; brush it off. Don't spray degreaser directly into wheel bearings, bottom brackets or headsets. It eats grease wherever it finds it, so if it does seep into bearings, you must strip them out and regrease them – a boring task. Also keep degreaser clear of suspension seals. Use a chain-cleaning box to keep the fluid contained.

◆ **Hand cleaner**. Essential! Most jobs start with a dirty procedure (like taking off an old broken part) and end with a clean one (such as adjusting a newly fitted part). Trying to assemble parts with new grease and dirty hands is a waste of time, so you need to be able to wash your hands in the middle of a job as well as at the end. Most hardware and car parts shops sell cleaner that's specially designed for oily hands. You'll also need plenty of cotton rags. The best source of this is often charity shops.

They usually have bags of T-shirts they can't sell as clothes, which make perfect rags. A sponge is better for paintwork than a brush.

Lubricant and grease

◆ **Chain lubricant**. This is an absolute essential. Everybody has a favourite type: with me it's Finish Line Cross-Country. Ask the mechanics in your local bike shop what they use. Different lubricants work in different climates. If you ride in a very wet and muddy place, you'll need a different lubricant from someone that rides in hot, dry climates. A dry climate requires a dry lubricant to keep the drivetrain running smoothly while attracting minimal muck. In muddy, wet conditions, you need a wet lubricant. These are stickier so they stay on in extreme conditions, but attract more dirt so you must be conscientious in your cleaning routine.

The important thing about chain lubricants is that they should be applied to clean chains. Putting oil on a dirty chain is the first step towards creating a sticky paste that eats expensive drivetrain components for breakfast. If you haven't got time to clean your chain first, you haven't got time to oil it. Whatever you use for oiling the chain will also do as a more general-purpose lubricant for cables, brake pivots, and derailleur pivots – anywhere two bits of metal need to move smoothly over each other.

I always use drip oil rather than spray oil. Spray is messy and wasteful, and it's too easy to get it on rims and disc rotors by mistake, which makes your brakes slippery rather than sticky. Your bike will be healthier if oil is delivered accurately to the places that need it the most.

◆ **Grease**. Confusion surrounds the difference between grease and oil. Essentially, they're both lubricants, but grease is solid and oil is liquid. Grease is stickier and can't be used on exposed parts of the bike; dirt sticks to the grease, forms a grinding paste and wears out the bike rather than making it run more smoothly. Grease is used inside sealed components like hubs. You don't get in there often so the stuff is required to last longer and remain cleaner. In an emergency almost any grease will do, but as you don't need much, get the good stuff from your local bike shop.

As your confidence grows, invest in a grease gun. This will keep your hands and grease stock clean.

For a clean and simple system, I like the ones that screw onto the top of a tube of grease. To get the last bit out, though, you usually abandon the gun and cut open the tube.

Specific lotions

As with your toolkit, start with a stock of essential items and build up as you tackle specialist jobs.

◆ **Disc brake fluid**. Use only the fluid specified for your brake system. DOT fluid, an autoparts trade standard, deteriorates once the bottle has been opened so buy in small amounts and open as you need it.

◆ **Suspension oil** is formulated to have damping properties. Its "weight" is critical and depends on the make and model of your fork or rear shock. Damping occurs by oil being forced through small holes. Lighter, thinner oil (e.g., 5wt) passes through more quickly. Heavier, thicker oil (e.g., 15wt) takes longer. Your fork or shock only works properly with the correct weight of oil: check the manual (which is, of course, neatly filed in your workshop!).

◆ **Antiseize** (also called Ti-prep). This prevents reactive metals from sticking together and is especially important for titanium components, which react and seize whatever they touch. Avoid skin contact with antiseize; this stuff is not good for you.

◆ **Vaseline** is often the best substance for applying to seatposts in carbon frames. Check with the frame manufacturer's recommendations.

◆ **Plastic components**. These need their own lubricants. SRAM Twistshifter gear-changers and the Sachs equivalent, Twistgrips, have to be cleaned with a suitable degreaser (e.g., Finish Line Ecotech) or warm soapy water, and oiled with a special plastic lube (e.g., Jonnisnot).

◆ **Loctite glue**. The generic name is threadlock, although the Loctite brand is pretty good. Used where bolts cannot be allowed to rattle loose and between parts that may corrode together if moisture gets in, like rear hubs. Different colours indicate different strengths. Threadlock "#222" is red and is usually applicable up to M6 (6mm diameter) threads. Threadlock "#242", the most common, is blue and used for bolts M6 and above. Threadlock "#290", for holding pivot bushes, is green.

Rescue Repairs

Your routes may take you far off the beaten track into remote areas, where the ability to carry out basic maintenance will make you much more self-sufficient. Sometimes, a really simple repair can make the difference between a great ride, where you had to stop and fix your bike in the middle, and a really tedious day when you had to walk home from the furthest point. Once you've learned how to fix your own bike, you'll be able to fix other peoples' as well – and once they realize you're handy with your toolkit, they'll think twice before leaving you behind on a ride.

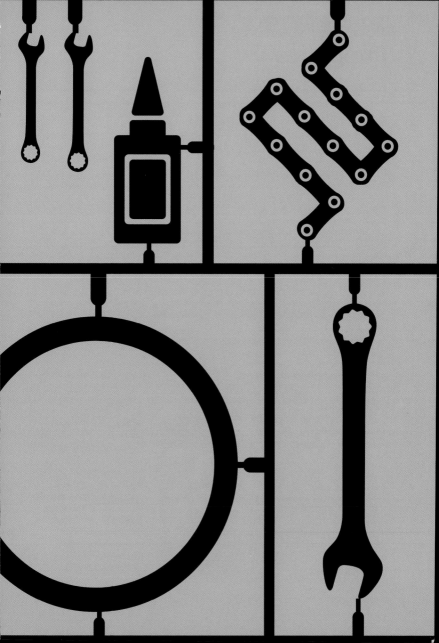

Punctures

Punctures are inevitable. The pressure inside the tyre is higher than the pressure outside, and the world is full of sharp things. Don't worry if you've never fixed a flat before though; it's not as difficult as people make out. And, like learning to tie your shoelaces, it gets easier with practice.

There are ways to reduce the number of punctures you get. Occasionally you pick up a sharp object that cuts straight through tyre and tube and causes a flat, but often objects take a while to work their way through the casing of the tyre. Before you set out, check both tyres: raise each wheel off the ground in turn, spin each slowly, and pick out foreign objects. Maximum and minimum pressures are printed or stamped on the tyre sidewall. Make sure the tyre is inflated to at least the minimum suggested pressure to reduce the chance of snakebite flats (caused when pressure from, say, a rock edge, squeezes two symmetrical holes in the tube against the sides of the rim). If you like riding at very low pressure, choose a tyre designed to take it. These tyres have a thicker sidewall, which won't fold over itself and pinch the tube.

Problems with punctures at, or around, the valve can also be caused by low tyre pressures. If there isn't enough air in it, the tyre will creep gradually around the rim, dragging the tube with it. The valve is held in place in the valve hole, so the tube around it becomes stretched and tears easily, ripping the valve out of the tube. Check your tyres regularly for large cuts as well – under pressure the tube will bulge out of these cuts and burst instantly. Some people suffer from punctures more than others. If you feel unfairly cursed, consider investing in puncture-resistant tyres. These have an extra layer of tough material incorporated into the carcass of the tyre under the tread, which helps to stop sharp things working their way through.

REPLACING TUBES

◀ **Step 1:** If you have rim brakes, you need to release them to get the tyre out easily. For V-brakes, pull the black rubber boot off the end of the noodle, squeeze the brake units together, and pull the noodle out and then up to release it from its nest. For cantilever brakes, squeeze the brake units together and push the cable nipple down and out of the slot in the unit.

◀ **Step 2:** Turn the bicycle upside down. Undo quick-release skewer. Unless you have a fancy skewer set, do this by folding (not turning) the handle over the axle. If you're unsure how to use quick-releases safely, read the section on them before you go any further (page 45). For the front wheel, undo the nut on the opposite side of the wheel several turns to get past the dropout tabs.

◀ **Step 3:** The rear wheel is a little trickier to remove than the front. Stand behind the bike. With your left hand, pull the body of the derailleur backwards with your fingers, and push the cage forwards with your thumb, as shown. This creates a clear path, so that you can lift the rear wheel up and forwards, without getting tangled up in the chain.

◀ **Step 4:** Inspect the outside of the tyre before you go any further to see if you can work out what caused the puncture. There may be nothing – you may have had a snakebite puncture or the escaping air may have ejected whatever caused the puncture. If you find something sharp, pry it out.

◀ **Step 5:** If there's any air left in the tyre, expel it. Remove the valve cap. For Presta valves (long and thin), undo the little thumb nut on top of the valve and press it down. For Schraeder valves (short, fat, car-tyre type), use something sharp, like a key, to push down the pin in the middle of the valve. The more air you get out of the tube at this stage, the easier it is to get the tyre off.

◀ **Step 6:** Each side of the tyre is held on by an internal wire, or Kevlar hoop, called the bead. To remove the tyre, lift enough of the bead over the sidewall of the rim. With care, this can be done by hand. Hold the wheel upright facing you. Work around the tyre, pushing the side closest to you into the dip in the middle of the rim. This will give you enough slack to pull the bead off.

◀ **Step 7:** With the wheel still upright and facing you, pinch a 10cm (4 inch) section of the side of the tyre nearest you with both hands. Lift this section up and over the rim, towards you. Hold it in place with one hand, and work gradually around the tyre with the other, easing the bead over the rim. Once you've got about a third of the tyre off, the rest will come away easily.

◀ **Step 8:** If you can't get the tyre off by hand, you need to use tyre-levers. Starting opposite the valve, tuck one lever under the bead in line with the spokes. Fold it back and hook the lever under the spoke to hold it in place. Move along two spokes and repeat with a second lever, then repeat with a third lever. Remove middle lever, leapfrog one of the others and repeat.

◀ **Step 9:** If the valve has a little nut screwing it to the rim, undo it. Reach inside the tyre and pull out the tube. Leave the other side of the tyre in place.

Toolbox

- **Spare tube** – check that the valve matches the tubes on your bike
- **Puncture kit** – backup in case you get more than one puncture
- **Pump** – make sure it works on your valve type. A pressure gauge is useful
- **Tyre-levers** – two is standard, take three if you're not confident
- **Spanners** – any spanners you need to remove your wheels
- **Tool pack** – carry these separately, so you can find them quickly
- **Warm clothes** – a hat to put on to keep you warm while you fix your bike – I get cold very quickly as soon as I stop riding

Refitting a new tube

It's vital to work out what caused the puncture before you fit a new tube. If the problem's still there when you fit a new tube, you'll puncture again right away – which is even more irritating if you haven't got a second spare tube.

Your first step is to inspect the tyre carefully. Look around the outside for thorns, shards of glass or sharp stones. If you can't see anything from the outside, check the inside of the tyre too. The easiest way to locate the culprit is to feel around inside the tyre with your fingers, moving slowly and carefully to avoid cutting yourself. If you're still unsure what caused the flat, pump air into the tube and locate the hole. You may be able to hear it rushing out of a big hole. Smaller holes can be harder to find – pass the tube slowly through your hands so that you can feel the air on your skin. You can put the tube in a bowl of water and watch for bubbles, but I don't usually carry a bowl of water in my emergency toolkit. Sometimes you can use puddles as an alternative. Once you've found the hole in the tube, hold the tube up to the tyre to locate the area of the tyre where the puncture occurred, and inspect the tyre again carefully.

Remove anything that you find. You won't necessarily find something in the tyre because punctures happen in other ways too. Pinch punctures – also known as snakebite flats – happen when you don't have enough tyre pressure. If you hit a rock hard the tyre squashes, trapping the tube between the rock and your rim. Pinch flats are usually easy to identify: you have two neat holes in your tyre, a rim width apart. Check the tyre sidewalls as well because a hole here will turn into a fresh puncture immediately. Big tears or gashes in the tyre will need to be repaired before you fit a new tube. Duct tape is ideal for smaller holes.

FITTING THE NEW TUBE

◀ **Step 1:** Now for the new tube. Remove the nut on the valve, if there is one. Pump a little air into the tube – just enough to give it shape. This will prevent the tube getting trapped under the bead as you refit the tyre. Pull back the section of tyre over the valve hole and pop the valve through the hole. Work around the tyre, tucking the tube up inside it.

◀ **Step 2:** Returning to the opposite side of the valve, gently fold the tyre back over the rim. This gets tougher as you go. When there's just a short section left, you'll get stuck. Push the sections of tyre you've already fitted away from the sidewall of the rim and into the dip in the middle, like you did to get it off. You should then be able to ease the last section on with your thumbs.

◀ **Step 3:** If you can't hand-fit the last section, use tyre-levers. Work on short sections 5cm (2 inches) at a time. Take care not to trap the tube between the rim and the tyre-lever as it's easy to pinch-puncture it. Once the tyre is reseated, push the valve up into the rim so that it almost disappears (to make sure the area of tube near the valve is not caught under the tyre bead).

◀ **Step 4:** Pump up the tyre. If you had a snakebite flat last time, put in a little more air. Once the tyre is up, retighten the thumb nut on Presta valves, screw the stem nut back onto the valve stem, and refit the dustcap. Don't fit the valve stem nut until the tube is inflated, as you risk trapping a bulge of the tube under the tyre bead.

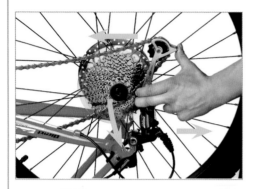

◀ **Step 5:** Rear wheel: with the bike upside down, stand behind it and hold wheel in your right hand. Put a left-hand finger in front of the guide jockey wheel (nearer the ground in this position), and your thumb behind the tension jockey wheel. Pull finger back and push thumb forwards, then place wheel so sprockets are within the loop of the chain. Guide the axle into the dropouts and secure.

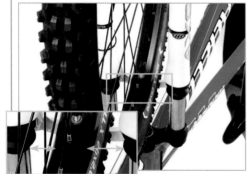

◀ **Step 6:** Refit the front wheel. This is easier. Drop the wheel into the dropout slots; make sure there's an equal amount of space between the tyre and the fork legs, and tighten the quick-release lever securely.

◀ **Step 7:** For disc brakes, wiggle the rotor (A) into place between the brake pads before settling the wheel into the dropout slots. You need to check that the rotor is sitting centrally between the brake pads inside the calliper. If it's hard to see, hold something light-coloured on the far side of the calliper. You may need to adjust the position of the wheel slightly so that the rotor is central.

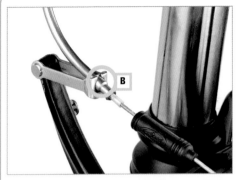

◀ **Step 8:** For rim brakes, don't forget to refit the brakes – it's easy to overlook this vital stage in the excitement of fixing your puncture. Pull the brake units together and refit the cable. If you have V-brakes take care to seat the end of the noodle (B) securely in the key-shaped nest.

◀ **Step 9:** Turn the bike back over and check that the brakes work: pull the front brake on and push the bike forwards. The front wheel should lock and the back one should lift off the ground. Pull the back brake on and push the bike forwards. The back wheel should lock, sliding across the ground. Lift up the wheels and spin them. Check that rim brakes don't rub on tyre.

Checklist: what caused the puncture?

- Sharp things (thorns, glass, flint) cutting through the tyre
- Cuts or gashes in the tyre that allow the tube to bulge out – check both the sidewall and the tread
- Snakebite punctures – when the tyre, without enough air, gets trapped between the rim and a rock
- Rim tape failure – when sharp spoke ends puncture the tube or when the tube gets trapped in rim holes
- Valve failure – when under-inflated tyres shift around on the rim
- Badly adjusted rim brakes – when blocks are set too high

Mending a broken chain

After punctures, repairing a chain is the most common trailside task. Chains get damaged by rocks and pebbles flicking up and trapping between chain and sprocket (gear ring). A mistimed or clumsy shift of the gears can have the same effect, putting pressure on the chain when it's stretched. Old, worn and neglected chains develop weak spots over time and are more likely to let you down under pressure.

For any kind of chain problem you'll need a chain tool. These are annoying to carry because they only do one job. But when you have a broken chain nothing else will do – if you haven't got one, you're walking home. It can be shocking when a chain breaks – one moment you're stamping hard on the pedals, the next moment all resistance is gone and you're left with spinning feet and no balance.

Your first step is to go back and retrieve the chain. They usually unroll in a straight line in the direction you were travelling, so if your chain is not immediately obvious, walk back parallel to the way you came and check your path. If you were moving fast it may be some way back.

Checking a repaired chain

Once you've finished rejoining the broken parts it's important to check that the repaired chain is still long enough to reach all the way around your drivetrain. It will be slightly shorter, since you will have removed damaged links. It is essential that there is still enough slack in the chain even in the largest sprocket, so that the derailleur is not strained or twisted. Otherwise, you risk tearing the derailleur off, damaging both the derailleur and the part of the frame to which it attaches.

Get someone to lift up the back of the bike for you, then change into the smallest sprocket at the back and the largest chainring at the front – pedal with your left hand and change gears with your right. Then change gears click by click towards the largest sprocket at the back, while watching the derailleur. As you move into larger sprockets, the derailleur will get stretched forwards. Check the tension of the lower section of the chain where it passes from the bottom of the chainring to the rear derailleur. If this section becomes tight, stop shifting. If you force the chain into a larger sprocket once the chain is tight, you'll damage the derailleur.

If the derailleur is struggling to reach the largest sprocket at the back, it's important not to change into this gear as you ride along.

Try to remember not to use this gear. Personally, I prefer to readjust the end-stop screw on the rear derailleur so that I cannot accidentally change into the largest chainring, because it's all too easy to forget once you start riding.

Shift click by click into larger gears until the chain becomes taut, then screw in the "low" end-stop screw until you can feel resistance – it will touch the tab inside the derailleur that limits further movement.

Once you get home, replace the chain with a new, longer one (you'll almost certainly need a new cassette too) and readjust your end-stop screw, so that the chain reaches the largest sprocket.

MENDING A CHAIN

Wide segment

Narrow segment

One link

◀ Step 1: Once you have the chain, look at both ends. One will be a narrow segment of chain and the other a wide segment. A complete link consists of one wide and one narrow segment. You will usually find that the plates on the wide segment got twisted and damaged as the chain broke, so this complete link (the damaged wide one plus the narrow one adjacent to it) has to be removed.

◀ Step 2: Look carefully at the chain to choose the right place to break it. When you come to rejoin it, you need to match up a narrow and a wide segment. Once you've selected the correct rivet, lay the chain over the chain tool as shown. Your chain tool probably has two sets of supports to lay the chain over. Choose the set furthest from the handle of the tool.

◀ Step 3: Turn the handle of the tool clockwise, so that the pin approaches the chain. When you get close, line up the pin very carefully with the centre of the chain rivet. If the pin is not properly aligned with the rivet you risk damaging the chain plates – creating a new weak spot on your chain – as you push the rivet out.

◀ **Step 4:** As you rotate the handle of the chain tool it will start to push the rivet out of the chain. Be careful how far you push the rivet through. If the chain is a Shimano – and you have a replacement rivet – push the old rivet all the way out. However, with other makes of chain you reuse the original rivet and must make sure you don't push it out completely because they're awkward to replace.

◀ **Step 5:** Ideally, you need to stop pushing the rivet when there's a little stub poking out just this side of the outer plate, well before it falls out. With a Park tool, wind the handle in until it won't go any further – this is exactly the right amount. You'll have to flex the chain slightly, as shown, to free the inner segment from the stub of rivet sticking out, then separate the chain.

One link

◀ **Step 6:** You'll have to take out a complete link – one wide section and one narrow section – so repeat the process, two rivets along, on the other side of your twisted link. You should now have a broken link and a slightly shortened chain; one end should end in a wide segment, the other in a narrow segment. Turn it so that the rivet at the wide end faces towards you.

◀ **Step 7:** Feed the end of the chain with the narrow segment between bottom tension jockey wheel and the tab at the bottom of the derailleur, then between the top tab and the top guide jockey wheel. If you have another bike, use it as a reference. Pass the chain around the front of the guide jockey, then over and back to the bottom of the cassette.

◀ **Step 8:** Continue behind the bottom of the cassette, up and forwards over the top and then towards the chainset. Pass the chain through the front derailleur. It will eventually have to sit on the chainrings but, for now, pass it around the front of the chainset, then drop it into the gap between the chainset and the frame to give yourself enough slack to rejoin the chain easily.

◀ **Step 9:** If you're refitting a standard chain, ease the two ends together, flexing the chain so you can slide the inner segment of chain past the stub of rivet sticking through to the inside of the outer plates. Once you've got it, though, the stub will make it easy to locate the rivet in the hole in the inner plates, lining the two ends of the chain up.

◀ **Step 10:** Lay the chain over the chain support furthest away from you. Turn the handle clockwise until the pin on the chain tool almost touches the rivet on the chain. Wiggle the chain to precisely line up the pin with the rivet.

◀ **Step 11:** Keep turning the handle, while pushing the rivet into the chain, until there is an even amount of rivet showing on both sides of the chain. Remove the tool.

◀ **Step 12:** Rejoining the chain usually squashes the plates together and makes the link stiff – see page 40 to remedy. Finally, reach around behind the chainset and lift the chain back onto a chainring. Stand up, lift the saddle up with your left hand and push the pedal around with your right foot so that the chain can find a gear.

Shimano chains

Shimano chains need to be treated slightly different from standard chains. The rivets that join each link are very tightly fitted together, so it will usually damage the chain plates if you try to reuse an original one.

When splitting and rejoining a Shimano chain the rivet must be pushed all the way out, then it has to be replaced with a special Shimano joining rivet.

The rivets are different lengths to match the different chain widths used by eight- and nine-speed systems, so make sure to choose the correct replacement: the longer eight-speed rivets are grey, the shorter nine-speed version is silver.

The replacement rivet is twice as long as the original rivets and has a groove in the middle. The first section is a guide to locate the rivet correctly in the chain and must be broken off once the second part of the rivet has been driven home with the chain tool. This means you need pliers to snap the guide off, as well as a replacement rivet.

Shimano chains are not designed to be used with Powerlinks, Superlinks or similar – they must only be fixed by replacing a rivet that has been removed with the special Shimano joining pin.

If you look carefully, you will see that each of the wider chain links is carefully shaped, with a bulge at either side.

These help the chain to lift easily onto a new sprocket when changing gear at the back, and a new chainring when changing gear at the front.

As with other brands, don't be tempted to patch together a chain with scraps from other makes – or to add new bits of chain into an old chain to make it longer. This will not work for one simple reason: the mismatched sections won't mesh properly with your sprockets, causing excessive chainwear and possible chainsuck.

REFITTING A SHIMANO CHAIN

◀ **Step 1:** Push the ends together until the holes line up, then push through the replacement rivet. The first half of the rivet goes through easily, holding things together while you use the chain tool. Lay the chain on the furthest supports of the chain tool, and turn the handle of the tool clockwise until the second half of the rivet begins to emerge.

◀ **Step 2:** Snap off the section of rivet sticking out, ideally with pliers. If you don't have any, trap the end of the rivet between two Allen keys on a multitool and twist.

◀ **Step 3:** Wriggle the new link. Often it is stiff because the plates get stuck together. Lay the chain back over the chain tool with the stiff rivet in the set of supports nearest the handle. Wind the handle in until the pin touches the rivet, then a further third of a turn to loosen link. Reach in behind chainset and lift chain back onto a chainring.

Successful chain-fixing – key points to note

- Always use a good-quality chain tool. Modern chains are made so that the rivet is a very tight fit in the chain plate. This helps to stop you from breaking them, but means that they will laugh at anything less than a proper chain tool.
- Big multi-tools sometimes include a chain tool. These are always better than nothing, but seldom as good as a proper separate one.
- Align the pin of the chain tool very carefully with the centre of the rivet, otherwise you risk damaging the chain plates and mangling the link.
- Always check links that you've just joined. They'll often be stiff because the chain plates get squashed together as you push the rivet through them. See page 40 to remedy.

Shortening chain to singlespeed

If you destroy your rear derailleur in a crash you are forced to run your chain on a single sprocket because you can no longer change gear. This repair tends to be more successful on hardtails (suspension forks only) than on full-suspension bikes, depending on how much of an effect the movement of the suspension has on the length of the chain. If you have to shorten the chain on a full-suspension bike you have to measure the length of the chain that you need with the suspension at its full extension.

The first task is choosing a suitable gear. The one with the best chance of success is the middle chainring at the front and the smallest sprocket at the back. Choose a random place in the chain and use the chain tool to split the chain, as shown on page 32. Remember to leave a stub of rivet sticking out to locate the hole in the rejoined chain later. Separate the two ends.

Unthread the chain from the rear derailleur and reroute it to pass through the front derailleur around the chainring of choice, back around a sprocket on the cassette while bypassing the rear derailleur altogether, and then forwards to meet up with the other end of the chain. Match up the ends and choose

where you're going to shorten the chain. Finding the perfect spot is sometimes tricky, but it's better to end up with a slightly slack chain than one that is too tight and binding. A binding chain will probably just break again.

Rejoin the chain, using the instructions on page 32. You have to ride carefully to keep the shortened chain in place without the tension from the rear derailleur, a component you don't notice until it's gone. Keep up an even pedalling pressure and don't be tempted to stand up on the pedals, because the extra jerkiness often throws the chain off.

Remember to save the section of chain you had to remove – you'll need to reuse it once you've repaired or replaced your derailleur. Chains and cassettes wear into each other with the chain stretching at the same rate the teeth wear, widening the valleys between teeth. You cannot just replace a chain, or a section of it, with a new chain without replacing your cassette at the same time. Your new chain will just skip and slip on the old cassette.

◀ **Route the chain around the smallest sprocket, bypassing the rear derailleur**

Stiff links/split links

You feel a stiff link as you're riding along – the pedals slip forwards regularly, but at different places in the pedal revolution.

To find a stiff link, change into the smallest sprocket at the back and the largest chainring at the front. Lean the bike up against a wall and pedal backwards slowly with your right hand. The chain heads backwards from the top of the front chainring, around the smallest sprocket, around the front of the guide jockey and the back of the tension jockey. Then it heads to the

front chainring again. The chain is straight as it travels across the top, then bends around the sprocket. The links should be flexible enough to straighten as they emerge from the bottom of the sprocket, then bend the other way to pass round the guide jockey. A stiff link won't straighten out as it drops off the bottom of the cassette and passes clumsily around the derailleur.

REPLACING STIFF LINKS

◀ **Step 1:** Once you've identified the problem link, get your chain tool out. You need to use the set of supports nearest the handle – the spreading supports. Look carefully at the problem rivet to identify whether one side of the rivet sticks further out one side of the chain than the other. If it is uneven, start with the sticking-out side. If it looks even, start with either side.

◀ **Step 2:** Lay the chain over the supports and turn the handle clockwise until the pin of the chain tool almost touches the rivet on the chain. Wiggle the chain to precisely line up the pin with the rivet. Turn until you can feel the pin touching the rivet, then just a third of a turn more. Back off the tool and wiggle it to see if the link is still stiff. Repeat if necessary.

◀ **Step 3:** If you don't have the chain tool with you, hold the chain as shown and flex it firmly backwards and forwards between your hands. Stop and check frequently to see if you've removed the stiff link. The last thing you want is to go too far and twist the chain plates.

Split links

A split link, also called Powerlink, is a quick and easy way to split and rejoin chains. It is particularly useful if you like to remove your chain to clean it, since repeatedly removing and replacing the rivets in chains can cause

weak spots. It's also a great emergency fix. You still need your chain tool for removing the remains of twisted or broken links, but the split link will not be stiff when you refit it and does not shorten the chain.

There are a couple of different types of split links; the best is the Powerlink, which comes free with SRAM chains. All split links work in similar ways.

The link comes in identical halves, each half with one rivet and one key-shaped hole. To fit, you pass a rivet through each end of the chain, linking the ends together through the wide part of the hole. When you put pressure on the chain it pulls apart slightly and locks into place. They never release accidentally.

To split the chain, locate the split link and push the adjacent links towards each other. The Powerlink halves are pushed together, lining up the heads of the rivets with the exit holes. You can then push the two halves across each other to release them.

◀ **Powerlink – the quick and easy way to split and rejoin chains**

Emergency wheel repairs

Wheels are excellent at resisting forces that are in line with them, like supporting your weight riding or jumping. However, they buckle easily under forces from the side, the kind of forces that are common when you crash.

A common disaster is crashing and folding either wheel so badly it won't turn between the brake blocks. The temptation is to release the offending brake and carry on riding, but clearly this is a bad idea – you're careful for 10 minutes, then you forget you only have one brake and pick up speed. And suddenly you've crashed again.

Use these pages to straighten your wheel by adjusting the tension in your spokes.

Your rim is supported all the way around by the tension in your spokes. The tension in each spoke can be increased or reduced by tightening (counterclockwise) (A) or loosening (clockwise) (C) the spoke nipple, effecting the short section of the rim to which the spoke is attached. Alternate spokes are attached to opposite sides of the hub. Tightening a spoke that leads towards the right-hand side of the hub will move the rim towards the right (B); loosening this spoke will allow the rim to move towards the left. Truing wheels is about

adjusting the tension in each spoke, so that the rim runs straight with no side-to-side wobble. This process is not the magic art that it's often made out to be – as long as you're careful about three things:

1) Spend a little time choosing the right spokes to adjust. Spin the wheel and watch the rim. Identify the section of the rim that is most bent – you may be lucky and have one single bent zone that you can concentrate on, but if the wheel is really buckled you will have to estimate where the centreline should be.

2) Working out in which direction to turn each spoke nipple is really tricky at first. Use the photo (left) as a guide. Watch the rim as you turn the nipple. If the bulge gets worse rather than better you're turning the nipple the wrong way.

3) Adjust the tension in each spoke in tiny steps. It's much better to work a quarter of a

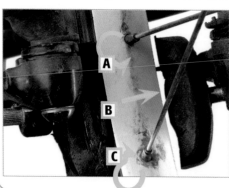

turn of the nipple at a time. Cranking the spoke key around in whole turns is a recipe for disaster. Adjust a quarter-turn, check the effect that you've had on the rim, go back and repeat if necessary.

Broken spokes

If you ride a wheel with a spoke missing, and don't straighten it, you will bend the rim permanently. Yet, as only long-distance riders heading for the Himalayas ever seem to carry spare spokes, there's a limit to what you can do if one does break. Rear wheel spokes can't be replaced unless you have the tools to remove and refit the cassette, making an emergency fix unlikely. But you can adjust the surrounding spokes to make the wheel as straight as possible, getting your brakes to work better (if you have rim brakes), and making it more likely you will be able to fix the wheel properly later.

First, render the snapped spoke safe by preventing it from wrapping around anything else. If it's broken near the rim, wind it around an adjacent spoke to keep it from rattling around. If it's broken near the hub, bend it in the middle so that you can hold it still. Use a spoke key to unwind the nipple so

that the spoke drops out of the end of the nipple. If it's broken in the middle, which is the least likely, do both.

Lift up the wheel and spin it gently to see how bent it is. There will usually be a single large bulge where the spoke is broken. Use a spoke key to loosen the spokes on either side of the missing one. It can be confusing working out which way to turn. Look at the spoke you want to turn and imagine you can see the top of the spoke nipple through the tyre. To loosen a spoke, turn it so that the top of the spoke head turns counterclockwise.

With rim brakes, check the clearance between brake blocks and tyre. You may find that the tyre rubs on the brake block in the broken spoke zone. If this is the case, loosen the Allen key bolt that holds the brake block in place, and move the block down slightly so that it clears the tyre. Retighten securely.

Straightening a bent wheel

With a spoke key you can sometimes get the wheel straight enough to ride safely. As a guideline, if the wheel has more than 2cm (1 inch) of sideways movement when you spin it, you are unlikely to be able to straighten it with a spoke key. One seldom

When to beat your wheel

There is an urban myth that you can straighten bent wheels by banging them on the ground, hard, at the point where they're bent. This myth is responsible for generations of gullible cyclists taking a slightly distorted wheel that could have been saved and beating it into a wreck.

The problem arises because there are, in fact, limited circumstances in which beating a wheel is worth a go. First, it must have a specific shape – it must look like a Pringle crisp, with exactly four evenly spaced bends, two in each direction. Second, the distortion must have been caused very recently. And third, the wheel must spring back into shape with exactly one firm tap. You will have a much higher chance of success (although, obviously, this takes all the fun out of it) laying the wheel flat on the ground and standing on the two high points. But don't try anything forceful at all. It usually doesn't work and is likely to make things worse – and more expensive to fix when you do get home.

appreciated advantage of disc brakes is that the brakes continue to work properly when the wheel is bent.

Turn the bike upside down. If it's the back wheel, get behind the bike; if it's the front, get in front so that you're in line with the wheel. Spin the wheel and look at the area where it passes between the brake blocks (or, if you have disc brakes, where brake blocks would be). If the wheel is too wobbly to pass between the brake blocks, release your brake units. If it's too wobbly to pass between the frame, pick your bike up and start walking home.

If you think you can straighten the wheel, spin it a couple more times and look at its shape. You need to identify the point where the wheel is most bent – the biggest bulge

away from the centre line. If you have V-brakes, use one of the brake blocks as a guide. Hold the brake unit still and spin the wheel, watching how the gap between the brake block and the rim changes. If the wheel is badly buckled you're going to have to make a rough judgment about where the centre of the wheel is, and work towards that. You won't get perfection in the field – just get it round enough to roll.

Adjustments of a quarter- or half-turn of the nipple are plenty. It's easy to start with a buckled but salvageable wheel and end up with a useless pretzel by going too fast. Much better to stick to small steps. Check the previous page if you're not sure which way to turn the nipple.

STRAIGHTENING A WHEEL

◀ **Step 1:** If you don't have V-brakes, you will have to improvise a gauge to measure the wobble of the wheel against. Zipties are invaluable here – either ziptie a stick to the chainstay or fork so that it sits level with the rim, or zip a tie around the fork or stay, leaving a long tag hanging off. Use the tag as your gauge.

◀ **Step 2:** Spin the wheel again and stop it when the middle of the biggest bulge is level with your gauge. Look at the spokes on the wheel. You'll see that alternate spokes lead to opposite sides of the wheel.

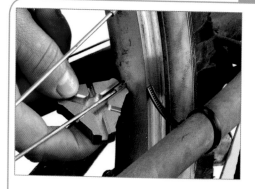

◀ **Step 3:** Choose the spoke at the centre of the bulge. If it leads to the same side of the wheel as the bulge, loosen this spoke and tighten the spokes on either side. A quarter- or half-turn should be enough. If the central spoke leads to the opposite side of the hub, tighten this spoke and loosen spokes on either side by a quarter- or half-turn. Spin the wheel again and pick out the biggest bulge.

Twelve routine safety checks before you ride

Checking your bike every time you ride it can seem like a lot of effort and a little bit boring. It needn't take more than a few moments, however, and occasionally you'll appreciate the time it takes because you'll pick up a problem waiting to happen, which is far easier to fix before you set off. Looking carefully at your bike regularly also makes it easier to spot when something is wrong.

It's worth having a routine for checking your bike. Doing it in the same order every time means you're less likely to miss something. It's worth going through a mental checklist at the same time to ensure you have everything else you need for a ride. Your needs will depend how far you intend to leave civilization behind, but normal items include plenty of water, emergency food, appropriate clothing, sunblock, map, tools and pump, as well as checking that somebody knows where you're going and when you are expected back. If you can rely on coverage,

a mobile phone can be invaluable in an emergency. It's not a substitute for careful preparation though.

1) **Quick-release skewer:** Check both wheels are securely attached. Quick-release levers must be firmly folded to line up with the fork blade or rear stay; otherwise they can snag on things and open accidentally. Most levers have "open" and "closed" printed on opposite sides. Fold the lever so the "closed" side is visible.

2) **Tyres:** Check tyres for bald patches, tears and sharp things. The glass and thorns, etc., which cause punctures often take time to work through the tyre casing. Inspect your tyres frequently and pick out foreign objects. It's tedious but quicker than fixing the punctures they cause!

3) **Spokes:** Check for broken spokes. Gently brush a hand over both sides of both wheels, with the ends of your fingers brushing the spokes. Even one broken spoke weakens a wheel considerably. A permanent repair is also much easier if the wheel hasn't been ridden on.

4) **Front wheel:** Lift front end of the bike off the ground and spin the front wheel. Check it runs freely and doesn't wobble between the forks.

5) **Rim brakes:** Check the brake blocks don't touch the tyre or rim as the wheel turns. Rubbing blocks wear quickly and slow you down. Check position of the brake blocks. Each block should be parallel to the rim, low enough to avoid hitting the tyre but not so low that any part of the brake block hangs below the rim. (N.B. Photo opposite is of a disc-brake bike.)

6) **Disc brake calliper:** Check disc pads. You should have at least 0.5mm ($\frac{1}{50}$ inch) of pad thickness on either side of both brakes.

7) **Brake lever:** Carry out a simple brake check every time you ride. Stand beside the bike, push it gently forwards, then pull on the front brake. The front wheel should lock on and the back one lift off the ground. If not, don't ride!

8) **Brake lever:** Use a similar test for the back brake. Push the bike forwards, then pull on the back brake. The back wheel should lock and slide along the ground. If not, do not ride.

9) **Chain:** Check the drivetrain. The chain should be clean and should run smoothly through the gears without falling off either side of the sprocket or the chainset. Turn pedals backwards and watch the chain run through the derailleur. Stiff links flick the derailleur forward as they pass over the lower jockey wheel. It's worth sorting them out since they can cause your gears to slip under pressure.

10) **Cables and hoses:** Check all cables (brake and gear) for kinks in the outer casing or frays in the cable. Check hydraulic hoses for links or leaks.

11) **Stem:** Check that stem and bars are tight. Stand over the front wheel, gripping it between your knees. Try turning the bars.

12) **Pedals:** Check the cleats in the pedals. Make sure you can clip into and out of both sides of both pedals easily.

Toolbox

Tools for three comfort zones
- 6mm Allen key to adjust saddle position
- 4 or 5mm Allen key to adjust saddle height (or quick release)
- 5 or 6mm Allen key to adjust bar and stem position
- 4mm Allen key to adjust cleat position

Tools for cleaning routine
- Muc-Off or bike wash
- Degreaser
- Stiff brush
- Sponge frame
- Chain oil to re-lubricate
- Plenty of warm water

Regular cleaning routine

Cleaning your bike is the best time to spot worn or broken parts. Beware of jet washes though. Power hoses can leave your bike looking very shiny without much effort, but, no matter how careful you are, they force water in through the bearing seals, flushing grease out. This shortens the lifespan of bottom brackets, headsets, and other components radically. As a principle, start with the dirtiest bits and work up to the cleaner ones. That way you minimize the amount of recleaning you may have to do.

◆ Start with the drivetrain: the chain, sprockets, chainset and derailleurs. If the chain isn't too dirty, clean it with a rag. See chain hygiene on page 84.

◆ If your chain is too oily and dirty to respond to this treatment, give it a thorough clean. You can do a very respectable job without removing the chain from the bike, which is a lot of trouble and can weaken the link you remove. For the best results with the least fuss, tip a little degreaser into a small pot. Use a toothbrush or washing-up brush dipped in degreaser to scrub the chain clean. A chain-cleaning box (see page 16) is a good investment, making this job cleaner and quicker.

◆ Sprockets and chainsets need regular cleaning too. They're close to the ground and exposed to whatever's going around. If they're oily and dirty, it's worth degreasing them. Oil is sticky and picks up dirt as you ride along, wearing out the drivetrain. As above, use a little degreaser and work it into the sprockets and chainset with a brush. It's very important to rinse things very carefully afterwards to remove all traces of degreaser. Also, dry components carefully. Be careful not to get degreaser into bearings.

◆ Once everything is clean and dry, relubricate the chain. I prefer drip oils to spray types because you can direct the oil more precisely. Drip a little onto the top links of the bottom stretch of chain all the way around. Don't use excessive amounts of oil. Leave the oil to soak in for five minutes, then carefully remove excess with a clean rag. Don't worry about relubricating other drivetrain parts as they need no more than is deposited by the chain onto the sprockets.

◆ Next, clean the wheels. Muddy tyres are best cleaned by riding your bike along a tarmac road (with your mouth shut) once the mud is dry. Use a sponge and bucket of warm soapy water, hold the wheels upright to keep water out of the hubs, and sponge the hubs and spokes clean.

◆ Rim brakes work much better on clean rims. They pick up dirt from the ground and from the brake blocks, which stops the blocks from gripping the rim effectively, causing both rims and blocks to wear out prematurely. Green nylon Brillo pads are ideal for this job. Wire wool is too harsh but nylon gets detritus off the rims without damaging the braking surface. While you're there, check for bulges or cracks in the braking surface. These indicate that the rim is worn out and needs replacing urgently. If your rim has rim-wear indicators, check them now too.

◆ Disc rotors, the alternative braking surface, also work much better when clean. It's important not to contaminate them with oil. Use Finish Line disc cleaner for disc rotors. If they are oily, clean the rotors with isopropyl alcohol (from a chemist), which doesn't leave a residue. Don't be tempted by car disc cleaner – this leaves a residue that cannot be scrubbed off by the brakes.

◆ Brakes next. For rim brakes, release the V-brakes by pulling back the black rubber boot and pulling the curved metal noodle out of the hanger on the brake unit. Clean the block surfaces. Use a small screwdriver or knife (carefully) to pick out shards of metal. If the block surface has become shiny, use a strip of clean sandpaper to roughen it. When looking at the brake blocks check they aren't excessively or unevenly worn. Most blocks have a wear-line embossed onto the rubber. If the blocks originally had slots, make sure the slots are still visible. Once they disappear it's time for new brake blocks.

◆ For disc brakes, wipe the calliper clean. Check hydraulic hoses for oil leaks. There should be no trace of oil at any of the connections. Also check for kinks in the hoses. Look into the rotor slot on the calliper and check that the brake pad is at least 0.5mm ($\frac{1}{50}$ inch) thick.

◆ Clean and oil the parts of your cables normally trapped inside casing.

◆ For rear cable brakes, follow the black casing back from the brake lever to the frame. At the cable stop, pull the casing forwards to release it from the cable stop and wiggle the brake cable out of the slot. Use the same method to release the other sections of casing.

Run a clean rag over the part that's normally covered by outer casing. Relubricate each section with a drop of oil. Refit the outer casing.

◆ Repeat with the gear casing. You need to click your rear shifter as if changing into the highest gear, then push the derailleur away again. This creates enough slack in the cable to pull a section of casing out of its cable stop. Repeat with all the other sections of casing, cleaning and oiling – especially the last loop of rear derailleur cable. This loop is nearest to the ground and tends to collect dirt. Refit the outer casing.

◆ Pull the front derailleur out over the largest chainring, click the shifter as if to change into the smallest sprocket, then release the casing in the same way. Clean, oil and replace.

◆ Pedals are often forgotten, even though they get more than their fair share of mud and abuse. Use a small screwdriver to clear all the mud from around the release mechanism. Make sure you do both sides of both pedals. Mud gets forced into the springs every time you clip in with your shoes, building up until you can no longer clip in and out properly. Lubricate the moving parts sparingly with a light oil, like GT85 or WD40.

Clean the frame and forks. You need a sponge and a bucket of warm water to rinse everything off afterwards. All components work better and last longer if they're not covered in grime. Finally, a quick polish. Wax-based polish helps stop dirt sticking to the frame, keeping it cleaner for next time. Saddles also benefit from a polish – you might as well while you've got the polish out. Refit the wheels, reconnect the brakes. This is a good time to pump up the tyres, just to finish the job off neatly.

Brakes

The brakes on your bike probably need more attention than all the other components put together. It's an inevitable part of cycling that you'll need to do lots of stopping and starting, and that some of this will need to be done in a very short distance at very short notice. Learning how your brakes work and how to adjust them means you can ensure they're always giving you as much control as possible. Constant use will wear your brakes out, giving you plenty of opportunity to practise replacing them.

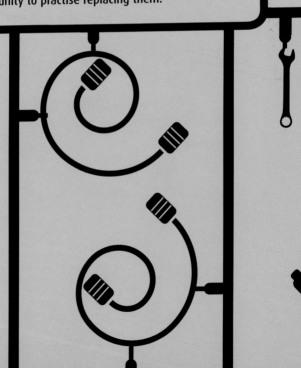

Brakes: build your stopping power

Well-tuned brakes make you go faster. This might seem like a contradiction, but it's true. In order to be able to go fast, you need to be able to control your speed safely. Crisp, reliable brakes will make you feel more confident and get you out of trouble when you push things too far.

Brakes are very satisfying to work on. Their performance tends to deteriorate slowly, with pads and cables getting slightly more worn and dirty with each ride, but not usually so suddenly that you notice them getting worse. The good thing about this is that when you come to fit fresh parts, or clean and service units and cables, your brakes will feel significantly better – always very satisfying!

Brakes are obviously a mission-critical safety component. Always check them very carefully after you've done any work on them

so that you can be sure you're safe to ride away. Make sure both brakes are working properly, then go back over all your nuts and bolts and check that you've tightened them all up. Anything that's left a little bit loose will rattle free as soon as you ride hard, likely leaving you in trouble.

Rim brake pads have universal fittings, but disc brake pads haven't settled down to a standard yet. Consequently, there are about 30 different patterns, with slightly different shapes, sizes and fittings. This is annoying as

V-brakes

Cable clamp bolt

Brake unit

Brake block adjusting unit

Brake block

Brake fixing bolt

the pads won't fit unless you get exactly the right kind. It's worth making sure you always have a spare set so you don't get caught out.

Cable brakes are simpler to deal with than hydraulic ones, but the extra braking power you get from the hydraulics makes them well worth learning about. Dealing with brake fluid can seem a bit of a leap into the unknown, even if you feel very confident working with other parts of your bike. But it's not really significantly more complicated than other tasks, just a bit different. Treat brake fluid – whether it's DOT or mineral oil – with respect: it's not good for your skin. Both fluids will contaminate brake pads, causing them to have trouble gripping the rotors properly. DOT will also strip the paint off your frame if you spill it. Wear gloves, and work slowly and patiently.

Cantilever brakes

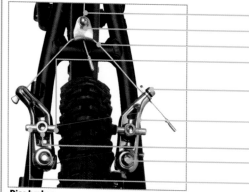

Brake cable

Straddle hanger

Straddle cable

Brake block

Cable bolt

Brake unit

Eye bolt

Brake fixing bolt

Brake block stub

Disc brakes

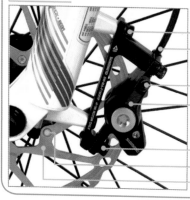

Calliper fixing bolt

Brake hose

Bleed nipple

Brake calliper

Calliper fixing bolt

Rivets to centre lock mount

Rotor

V-brakes: a general introduction and how to manage wear and tear

V-brakes have now become standard issue on mountain bikes. They have superseded cantilever brakes and will in turn be made obsolete by disc brakes. However, they are cheap and simple to maintain, so we will start with them. Here follows an outline of the advantages and disadvantages of this braking system.

V-brakes ousted cantilevers because they are more powerful, as well as being easier to adjust. However, there has always been a trade-off – cantilever pads last much longer. V-brakes stop you faster because the way they are designed pushes them onto the rim harder, wearing out both the rim and brake blocks faster. So, enjoy the powerful braking but remember that as a direct consequence you are going to have to learn to inspect brake blocks frequently for wear and replace them.

Regular maintenance

Keeping blocks and rims clean will make a huge difference to how long they both last. Dirty rims will wear out brake blocks, while flakes of grit and metal caught in your brake blocks will scour the rim surface. It's easy to forget that the rims are an integral part of the braking system. Unless they're clean and flat, the brake blocks will struggle to grip them and stop you in your tracks.

This section takes you through the processes of checking that your V-brakes are set up and working correctly, fitting new brake blocks, fitting a new cable and servicing your brake units. Careful brake-block alignment and smooth cables will help you get the most power out of your brakes. You'll also get more feedback from them. Good set-up means that when your hands are on the brake levers, you will be able to feel what effect the brakes are having, increasing your control over the bike. Good brakes don't just lock the wheel up, they allow you to control your speed accurately.

One important thing to remember is that brake blocks and cables often just need cleaning rather than replacing. Cables can be cleaned rather than replaced as long as they're not frayed or kinked. Use the following procedure for replacing your cable. Keep to the instructions for removing the old cable, then clean it with a light oil like GT85. If necessary, soak congealed dirt off with degreaser. Cut the end of the cable off cleanly so that it can be neatly threaded through the outer casing. Clean the inside of the outer casing by squirting spray oil through it to flush out dirt. Replace any sections that are cracked, squashed or kinked. Replace bent ferrules. Then refit as a new cable.

Worn-out brake blocks

Brake blocks must be replaced if they're worn below the wear-indication lines stamped on the block. If there are no wear lines, replace the brake blocks when you've worn down to the base of any grooves moulded into the block. They're also due for replacement if any of the metal over which the rubber block is moulded is showing through. Otherwise, they can be cleaned and freshened up. Follow the instructions for removing the blocks. Use a sharp knife to cut off overhanging lips at the edge of the brake block, and use clean sandpaper to flatten the braking surface of the block. Pick out any flakes of metal or grit. Refit as new brake blocks.

V-brakes are bolted onto your frame or forks by studs called brake pivots. Newer, disc-only frames and forks, as well as road bike frames, don't have these pivots, and so cannot be fitted with V-brakes. Currently, many new hybrid bikes have both disc mounts and V-brake pivots, allowing you to upgrade from V-brakes to discs.

The brake units are designed to rotate around the pivots so the condition of the pivots is important. If the surface is rusty or corroded, your brakes won't pull smoothly onto the rim or spring back smartly. If your brakes are sluggish and fitting a fresh cable has no effect, see page 67 to service your brake units, and to clean and oil the pivots.

Crashing can also bend the brake pivots, preventing you from adjusting them properly. Look at the brakes from face on: the front brake from in front of the bike, the rear brake from behind. You'll see the heads of the two brake-fixing units at the bottom of each unit. These should point straight out from the frame so that the bolts are parallel. Bent brake units don't just make it awkward to adjust the brake block position, they can also be a liability. Many fork pivots, and some frame pivots, can be replaced; check with the manufacturer for spares. Although, if you have disc mounts as well as V-brake pivots, this could be a good excuse for an upgrade.

V-brakes: a quick checkup to help ensure performance every ride

However casual you are about bike maintenance, you need to make sure that your brakes are working properly every time you set off on a ride. This doesn't need to be a lengthy procedure – just give your bike a careful visual check before you head off.

The steps below make up a quick and regular check to keep your brakes in good running order and they give you warning when it's time for a more serious overhaul.

If the steps on page 56 indicate any problems, please refer to pages 57–60 and 64–66 for relevant repairs. Whatever you do, don't set off on a ride with brakes that don't work properly.

Lift each wheel and spin it to check the brakes don't rub on the rims or the tyre as the wheel turns. Look at the gap between the brake block and the rim on each side of each brake. See page 57.

You'll need to disconnect the brake cable so that you can pull the brake blocks out from the rim. V-brakes are designed to make this easy. They also help when you want to remove and replace the wheels because you can get the tyre out past the brake blocks without letting the air out.

The brake cable

The brake cable arrives at the brake unit via a short curved metal tube called a "noodle" or "lead pipe" (pronounced as in "leading in the right direction", not lead, the heavy metal). The end of the lead pipe has a pointed head with a raised collar. The brake cable passes through the noodle and then clamps onto one of the brake units. The other brake unit has a hinged hanger with a key-shaped hole for the noodle.

The collar stops the noodle pulling through the hanger, so when you pull on the cable, the two brake units are drawn together, pulling the brake blocks onto the rim. The section of cable between the hanger and the cable clamp bolt is often concealed inside a black rubber boot that helps keep the cable clean.

To release the brake units, draw back the rubber boot to reveal the head of the noodle where it emerges from the hanger. Squeeze the two brake units together to create slack in the cable. Pull the noodle back and out of the key-shaped hole, then pull up to release the cable from the slot in the key-shaped hole. Let go of the brake units – they will spring right back from the rim.

To reconnect the brakes, squeeze the brake units firmly onto the rim. Pull back the rubber boot so that it's out of the way of the noodle and guide the head of the noodle into the hole in the hanger. Make sure it's seated securely: the raised collar must be butted firmly up against the hanger. Refit the rubber boot back over the head of the noodle. Pull the brake lever to confirm that everything is seated correctly.

CHECKING V-BRAKES

◀ **Step 1:** Inspect the condition of the pads. Release the brakes (see above), pull each side away from the rim, and check that each braking surface is flat, has nothing stuck in it and isn't worn through. Reconnect the brakes, checking that the brake noodle is firmly and securely located in its hanger..

◀ **Step 2:** Check that each block hits the rim flat, square and level. Brake blocks that are too high will cut through the tyre, causing explosive punctures. Blocks that are too low hang under the rim, wasting brake potential and creating a lip that eventually starts to snag on the rim.

◄ **Step 3:** Run your hand along each cable, from lever to brake unit, checking for corrosion, kinks, fraying or damage to the casing (A). Pull the lever firmly towards the bars and check that each brake locks the wheel when the lever is halfway to the bars.

Replacing and adjusting brake blocks

One of the points used to sell V-brakes originally was that changing the brake blocks would be easier than with cantilever brakes. This is slightly misleading – changing blocks is not difficult, but it can be fiddly. I often find myself wishing I had smaller fingers – or more of them.

Even if you don't wear out blocks very quickly you should still change them periodically as they harden with time and don't work as well. Every year should do.

In between full changes, check on the condition of the pad and improve it. This is easiest to do with the wheels removed.

Release the brakes and remove the wheel. Look at the condition of the pad. It should be flat and even, without visible contamination. If you can see flecks of meta, use a sharp knife to pick them out carefully. If the pad had been sitting too low or at an angle it will wear unevenly, leaving a lip that gets caught under the rim and prevents the brakes from

letting go properly. This is a waste of brake block and braking potential. Carefully cut the offending lip off with a sharp knife, then follow the instructions to reposition your brake block so that it contacts the rim more evenly. If the brake block sits too high, it will wear through the tyre – an expensive error.

Lightly sand the surface of the brake block with clean sandpaper. People often use a file for this, but shouldn't – it will hold metal flakes from whatever it was you last filed, and flakes will embed themselves in the blocks. Clean your rims too. If they have sticky black streaks, use degreaser. Oil or tar on your rims will squeal alarmingly, allowing your wheels to slip through the blocks without slowing you down. A green nylon scouring pad works well for stubborn stains, and will scrub off contamination without damaging your rims.

Some brake blocks are designed with removable rubber blocks. The old, worn ones are removed by pulling out a retaining pin at the back of the metal cartridge and sliding the rubber part backwards. Replacement rubber blocks slide in in the same way and are held in place with the retaining pin.

Always make sure the open end of the cartridge faces towards the back of the bike, otherwise heavy braking will rip the rubber out of the cartridge. The replacement blocks can be stiff to slide into the slots in the cartridge; it often helps to dip them in warm water.

CHANGING BRAKE BLOCKS

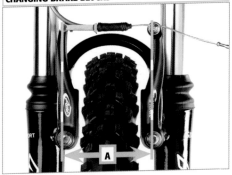

◀ **Step 1:** Undo and remove Allen key nut on the end of the old brake block stud, then wriggle out the old block and its curved washers. Now look at the position of the brake units. They should be parallel and vertical (A). Get the position of the units right before you fit new brake blocks. If they're not parallel, undo cable pinch bolt and pull in or release cable. Retighten the pinch bolts.

◀ **Step 2:** You may find the units are parallel but pointing off to one side. If so, use the balance screws at the bottom of each unit to even out the spring tension. This screw is normally a slot head but might be an Allen key. Choose the side that sits closer to the wheel and move screw half a turn clock-wise. Pull and release the brake to settle the spring and repeat until brake arms are even.

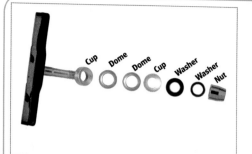

Cup Dome Dome Cup Washer Washer Nut

◀ **Step 3:** Check whether the brake blocks are designed for fitting in a particular direction. Any arrows should point forwards and the shape of the block should follow the curve of the rim. Each block comes with a collection of curved washers to space and angle the block. Their order of use varies from bike to bike and depends on the distance between the brake unit and the rim.

◀ **Step 4:** There should be a domed washer on the inside of the brake unit with the flat side facing the brake unit, and a cup washer between the dome and the brake block. Choose either the thick one or the thin one so that the block sits close to the rim, but not touching. A gap of about 2-3mm (around ⅛ inch) is ideal.

◀ **Step 5:** The adjustment does not need to be perfect at this stage, just approximate. With the stub of the brake block sticking out through the slot in the brake unit fit the other domed washer, flat side against the brake unit. Then fit the remaining cup washer, followed by any flat washers. Finally, loosely fit the Allen key nut.

◀ **Step 6:** You will find that with this arrangement you can alter the angle of the brake block and also slide it up and down in the slot in the brake unit. Set it so that when you pull on the brakes the block hits the rim with the fixing bolt at 90° to the surface of the rim. The block should be level and none of it should hang over the top or bottom of the rim.

◀ **Step 7:** "Toeing-in": the front of the block (B) should be 1mm (¹⁄₁₆ inch) closer to the rim than the back, facing the same direction as the bike. Toeing-in helps stop your brakes squealing. Position the block and tighten the fixing bolt firmly. Check you cannot twist the block; the bolt must be firmly secured! Fit the other block the same way.

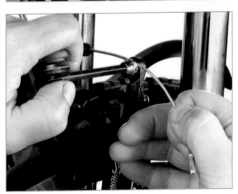

◀ **Step 8:** You will probably have to adjust the tension in the cable again to get the correct gap between brake blocks and the rim. For big changes undo the cable pinch bolt again, pull though or let out cable and tighten the pinch bolt. For a more subtle change use the barrel-adjuster on the brake lever.

The balance screw

Each V-brake unit has a balance screw. You'll find it at the bottom of the unit, usually a crosshead bolt but occasionally a small Allen key. The end of each bolt rests on the end of the brake-return spring, so that the spring is forced against the bolt when you squeeze the brake unit towards the rim.

Turning the balance screw alters the preload on the spring, pushing its starting point further around the unit for a stronger spring action and releasing it for a weaker spring action. The confusing part is remembering which way to turn the screws for the effect you need.

◆ Turning the balance screw clockwise (A) pushes it further into the unit, increasing the preload on the spring, making it springier and pulling the attached brake block away from the rim.

◆ Turning the balance screw counterclockwise (B) unscrews it from the unit, decreasing the preload, softening the spring and allowing the brake block to move nearer to the rim.

Since the two units are connected together by the cable across the top, adjusting one balance screw will affect both units: if one unit is pulled away from the rim, the other will be drawn towards it to compensate.

To adjust the balance screws, look first at each brake unit from face on – the front brake from directly in front of the bike, the rear brake from directly behind.

If the balance screws are badly adjusted the units will point off to one side, rather than being parallel and vertical. There will be an uneven distance between brake blocks and rim, perhaps with one closer than the other, or even with one brake block dragging on the rim. To correct the problem locate the balance screws. Start with the unit that's closer to the rim and wind the balance screw in (clockwise) a couple of turns. You'll need to squeeze and release the brake lever every time you make a balance-screw adjustment to resettle the position of the spring. Look again at the angle of the two units. You should find that the adjustment has both pulled the closer brake block away from the rim and pulled the other block closer.

One confusing thing about the balance screws is that turning the screw has a different effect at different points – sometimes a couple of turns seems to make no difference at all, sometimes a quarter-turn makes a radical change. You'll have to experiment, adjusting the balance screws a quarter-turn at a time.

◀ **Balance screws**

Readjusting balance screws

Finally, you will probably need to readjust the balance screws. Turn the balance screw clockwise to pull that side brake block away from the rim, but remember that this also pulls in the opposing brake block towards the far side of the rim. Pull and release the brake levers frequently as you adjust the balance screw because they have to settle into place every time. Check every nut and bolt to make sure each one is tight. Pull on the brakes firmly, and check that the wheel locks up. Spin the wheel and watch the brake blocks – if the wheel isn't completely true, you might find that the tyre rubs on the brake block as the wheel spins. Readjust the brake block position if necessary.

Choosing new brake blocks

This V-brake block set-up, using a threaded stud with curved washers, is used almost universally, making V-brake blocks completely interchangeable between makes and models. This might seem unremarkable but the situation with disc brake pads is completely different. Every make and model requires a specific pad – and nothing else will do. The interchangeability of V-brake blocks has helped to keep the price down, since each manufacturer knows you can go elsewhere for replacements. Good makes include Aztec, Fibrax and Shimano. Longer or fatter brake blocks won't give you more braking power but are more durable. Slots cut in the surface of the block can help channel water away, but they can also collect grit if not cleaned regularly. Ceramic-coated rims need matching ceramic-specific brake blocks, which are harder than standard ones. Normal ones will wear away very quickly, as will ordinary rims if you use them with ceramic blocks.

Possible causes if the brake blocks are rubbing

You may find that, even after careful adjustment, one block or the other continues to rub. The most common problem is a wobbly wheel – if the rim is out of true, it will change position relative to the brake blocks as it revolves. For small wobbles, it's ok to spin the wheel to estimate an average position, then adjust the brakes to that position.

For wobbles larger than 2mm (0.08 inch), the wheel will have to be trued before the brake blocks can be adjusted correctly.

Toolbox

Tools for adjusting balance screws
- Usually crosshead screwdriver, occasionally 2.5mm Allen key

Tools for fitting or servicing brake units
- 5mm Allen key for brake-fixing bolts
- Oil to lubricate pivots
- Wet-and-dry sandpaper to clean pivots and to roughen braking surface

Check rims regularly for wear and tear

It's easy to forget that the rims are just as much a part of the braking system as the brake blocks. Every time you brake you're forcing your brake blocks against your rims. Powerful, controllable braking depends upon the condition of both blocks and rims. Whenever you brake you wear both surfaces.

Rim design is subject to two competing demands. When you're trying to go faster, it helps to have rims that are as light as possible. Your wheels are spinning around as well as along, so saving weight on them makes the bike feel substantially faster than saving the same weight on a static part of your bike like the handlebars. Ideally, the rims should be as thin as possible so that they don't weigh much. Light wheels make it much easier for your bike to accelerate, as well as facilitating changes in direction when you're moving fast.

But when you're trying to slow down, you need the rim material to be thick because the action of braking wears it out – and you don't want the brake blocks to wear through the rim. The truth is that rim manufacturers make their rims light so you buy them, but they expect you to keep them clean, so they wear as slowly as possible and to inspect them regularly.

Rim sidewalls

Having a rim sidewall blow suddenly is very alarming. Because of the pressure inside the tyre, the sidewalls don't give way gracefully. Over time the sidewall gets thinner and thinner. One part of the sidewall gets too thin to hold in the tyre. Then you brake suddenly – the moment of reckoning! Once one section of the rim starts to give way it cannot support

the next section, so within a fraction of a second most of your sidewall is ripped off. This punctures your tube, the resulting mess usually jams on your brake and you fall off the bike.

Some newer rims come with indicator marks that show when the rim is worn out. The rim will have a small hole drilled from the inside but not all the way through. The position of the hole is marked by a sticker on the rim with an arrow pointing to where the hole will appear. As you wear away the sidewall, the bottom of the hole appears from the outside; you can see your tyre through it. Time to get a new rim!

If you don't have a wear-indicator check the condition of the sidewall by running your fingers over it. It should be flat and smooth, without deep scours and ridges. Check both sides because one sidewall may be far more worn than the other. Curvy, bulging or scarred rims are due for replacement. If they look suspect, ask your bike shop for an opinion. If you find any cracks in the sidewall when you inspect, stop riding immediately.

It's also worth checking the join where the two ends of the rim meet. Sometimes, the ends don't meet exactly, making a bump in the rim that knocks against the brake blocks. Also check for cracks around the spoke holes and the valve hole. These are less dangerous but still mean the rim should be replaced.

Maintaining your cables

You should check your cables regularly for corrosion, kinks and damage to the outer casing. Over time, dirt and water creep into the cables. It happens slowly so you hardly notice the brakes are getting harder to pull on and are not releasing properly. Fitting new cables is easy. You will feel the difference instantly.

Cables generally come in either standard or fancy versions. The luxury versions tend to be either lined or protected by a sheath that runs from shifter to brake. Luxury cables can make a significant difference if you ride in very muddy environments, as they stop grit from creeping into the gap between cable and outer casing. However, they are generally much more expensive. All cables come with comprehensive instructions though, so we'll stick to standard cables here. You can either buy brake-cable sets in a pack, with cable, outer casing and ferrules – Shimano make a good value pack – or you can buy the parts separately. Either way, you'll need a decent pair of cable-cutters to cut the casing to length; every bike has a different configuration of top tube lengths and cable-stop positions so the casing needs to be cut

for each one. The key thing to remember when cutting casing is to make a square cut across the tube so that the end of the casing sits firmly inside the ferrule. Look into the end of the cut casing and make sure there isn't a stray spur of metal across the hole. This will catch on the cable every time you pull and release the brakes, making your brakes feel sluggish. Use the sharp point of a knife to open out the end of the white lining that runs through the casing as it gets squashed shut as you cut the casing.

Fitting new brake cable

Before you start taking things apart, have a good look at how the cable is currently set up because you need to recreate that later with the new cable. Snip the cable end off the old cable and undo the cable pinch bolt.

FITTING BRAKE CABLE

◀ **Step 1:** Unthread the old cable from the brake noodle and all the way through the outer casing, leaving the casing in place. Turn the lockring on the barrel-adjuster and then the barrel-adjuster itself, so that the slots on both the barrel and the lockring line up with the slot on the body of the brake lever Then pull the cable gently outwards, or down, to release it.

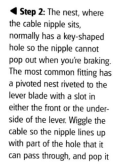

◀ **Step 2:** The nest, where the cable nipple sits, normally has a key-shaped hole so the nipple cannot pop out when you're braking. The most common fitting has a pivoted nest riveted to the lever blade with a slot in either the front or the underside of the lever. Wiggle the cable so the nipple lines up with part of the hole that it can pass through, and pop it

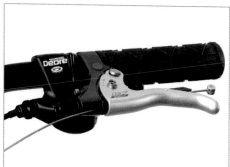

◀ **Step 3:** Some Shimano levers use a variation where the nipple is trapped behind a lip halfway along the lever blade. Once again, line up the slots on the lockring and barrel-adjuster with the slot on the body of the cable. You will need to flick open the plastic cover on the back of the lever blade, then push the cable towards the outer end of the lever.

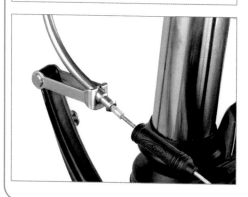

◀ **Step 4:** Once you've removed the old cable from the lever, replace it with the nipple from the new cable, then slip the cable back through the slots in the brake lever. Feed the cable back though the sections of outer casing with a drop of oil. Feed the cable through the V-brake noodle, and sit the noodle back into its key-shaped hole.

◀ **Step 5:** The cable normally clamps on above the bolt, but there will be a groove in the unit where you put the cable. Pull cable through, so there is a gap of 2-3mm (around $\frac{1}{8}$ inch) between brake blocks and rim. Steadying the cable with one hand, tighten the clamp bolt with the other. Leave about 5cm (2 inches) of exposed cable and crimp on a cable end behind the brake unit.

◀ **Step 6:** Test the brake; pull the lever hard twice. The cable might give slightly. Ideally, the brake should lock on when the lever is halfway to the handlebar. Use the barrel-adjuster to fine-tune; undo the lockring and turn it twice, away from the brake lever body. If the lever pulls too far turn the top of the adjuster towards the handlebars. Do a couple of turns and retest.

Replacing outer casing

If the new cable doesn't run smoothly through your outer casing it's worth replacing the casing – it could be dirty inside, or kinked. Replace one section at a time, so that you can use the old casing to measure new lengths. As you cut the casing, make sure the ends are neat and flat. Check that you haven't left a tang of metal across the cut end, and open out squashed lining with the point of a sharp knife. Each end of each section of casing will need a ferrule, apart from the last one that fits into the noodle – only fit one here if there's room for it.

Final adjustments

If you run out of adjustment on the barrel-adjuster (either it's adjusted so it jams on the brake lever body or it's at risk of falling off), go back to the cable clamp bolt, undo it, pull through or release a bit of cable, and retighten.

Then go back to the barrel-adjuster and make fine adjustments. Pull firmly on the brake lever again and check that it locks the wheel when it's halfway to the bar. Make sure that the brake blocks don't rub on the rims as the wheel turns. Check that every bolt is tight. You're done.

Fitting new v-brake units

V-brake units get very tired if you use them hard. Every time you pull and release the brakes, the units rotate around the pivots, bending then releasing the spring. The pivots and springs won't last forever, particularly if you ride in muddy or dusty conditions. Simple, single-pivot types (like the Avid units in the pictures, or the Shimano Deore types) tend to last longer than those with a complex multi-pivot arrangement.

All V-brake units are made to fit the same size and shape of brake pivot, so you can swap between makes and models without running into compatibility problems. New brake units are supplied with a set of new brake blocks. Once you take the price of these into consideration, a new set of brake units is a good-value upgrade.

Servicing V-brake units

Old brake units that are a bit tired can be revived with servicing. You'll need to release the brakes, then disconnect the cable clamp bolt. Undo and remove the fixing bolts at the bottom of each unit, then pull the brake units off the brake pivots. You may need to wiggle and pull at the same time, especially if the brake pivots have become corroded. Use a small brush (old toothbrushes are ideal) and degreaser to scrub all the dirt out from the gaps between the moving parts. Hold the unit still and wiggle the spring – if there's dirt in there, flush it out. You may find that you can pull the spring off the back of the unit. This makes it easier to clean behind, but remember to note the position and orientation of any washers or spacers.

It's best to work on one brake unit at a time; that way, you always have the other unit for reference if you get confused when reassembling the parts. Rinse the unit to get rid of residue from the degreaser, and oil the gaps between the moving parts. Move the spring against the unit to work the oil into the gaps, then wipe off the excess. Remove the cable clamp bolt and clean off any trapped dirt under the bolt head or the washer. Oil the threads of the cable clamp bolt and replace it. Clean the brake pivots carefully, removing any corrosion with wet-and-dry paper. Oil the pivots, then refit the brake units as above.

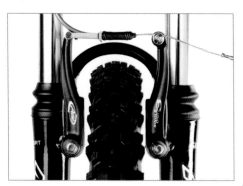

V-brake unit ▶

Cantilever brakes

You really don't see many cantilever brakes on mountain bikes nowadays, though they're still popular on cyclocross bikes (where they're not expected to actually stop you, but simply slow you down). They were the forerunners of V-brakes and whilst they've both now been surpassed in terms of power and practicality by the disc brake, cantilevers are still to be found on the steeds of those who lovingly restore 'retro' builds to their former glory – or who just still ride an old bike.

Take care to use the correct brake levers for cantilever brakes because they are not compatible with V-brake levers. V-brake levers are designed with a greater distance between the lever pivot and the nest that the cable nipple sits in. This means that more cable is pulled through the lever with V-brakes than with a cantilever brake lever. You can see the difference if you compare a V-brake lever to a cantilever brake lever. For a cantilever brake to work properly, the distance between brake lever pivot and cable nest needs to be around 30mm (1 ⅛ inches).

Cantilever brake blocks usually last much longer than V-brake blocks, but they will wear through eventually. Change them every couple of years whether they're worn down or not; the rubber hardens and ceases to work well after a while. This seems to be especially true if your bike lives outside or in outbuildings that get cold in the winter.

Check for wear by looking on top of the block for a wear-indication line. Usually stamped in black writing on the black surface of the block, they can be hard to spot, and you may be able to feel the line with a fingernail more easily than you can see it. There may not be an indication line; in this case, replace blocks before they've worn down to the base of the grooves moulded

into the blocks. Leave it too late and you risk wearing through to the metal bolt that the block is moulded around. The bolt will scrape the surface off your rims.

The brake block is held in place by an eye bolt. The stub of the brake block passes through a hole in the eye bolt, which in turn passes through a curved washer then through a slot in the brake unit. On the other side of the brake unit is another curved washer, then a nut. When you tighten the nut, it pulls the eye bolt through the brake unit, squashing the stub of the brake block against the first curved washer, and holding it securely.

This design means that when you loosen the nut on the end of the eye bolt, you can move the position of the brake block in different and useful ways. You can move the eye bolt up and down in the slot on the brake unit so that the brake block hits the rim higher or lower. You can push the stub through the eye bolt, moving the brake block towards or away from the rim. You can roll the stub in the eye bolt so that the block approaches the rim at an angle. You can also twist the eye bolt on the curved washers so that the front or the back of the brake block touches the rim first. We use this flexibility to get the block precisely positioned.

The vital adjustment for cantilever brakes

is setting the position where the main cable splits into two, just above the brake units. The split can be made with a straddle hanger bolted onto the cable, with a straddle wire that passes from one brake unit to the other via the straddle hanger, or with a separate link wire, through which the main cable passes, then clamps to the brake unit. Either way, it's important that the two sections of straddle cable, or the two arms of the link wire, are set at 90 degrees to each other. The best time to get this right is when fitting new brake blocks.

▼ Four degrees of freedom

Fitting and adjusting brake blocks

I find it easiest to work on one brake unit at a time, removing the old block then replacing it straight away with the new one. This way, you will keep the washers and eye bolt in the correct order. If you take both blocks off at once, the washers and eyebolt have a tendency to drop off one unit when you're working on the other.

Hold the eye bolt still using a 5mm Allen key in the head of the eye bolt, and undo the nut at the back of the unit. You don't need to take the nut off, just loosen it enough to pull the old brake block out. Feed the stub of the new brake block back through the hole in the eye bolt so that the brake block faces the rim. Most brake blocks will fit either way around, but if there are any arrows printed on the block, point these forward. If one end of the brake block is shorter than the other, this goes at the front.

FITTING BRAKE BLOCKS

◀ **Step 1:** Tighten the nut just enough so that the brake block doesn't fall out. Don't worry about adjustment at this stage, as long as the block is pointing vaguely towards the rim. Leave a generous gap between rim and brake block at this stage. Repeat with the other side. Now we're going to leave the brake blocks for a bit and set the units up at the right angle.

◀ **Step 2:** For straddle wire types, adjust the height of the straddle hanger and the length of the straddle wire, so that the two halves of the straddle wire are at 90° to each other. Link wire types are much simpler – undo the cable clamp bolt, pull in or let out until the two arms are at 90° and reclamp. Most link wires are stamped or printed with a helpful guide line.

◀ **Step 3:** Next, the balance screw. Cantilevers usually only have one. Pull brake lever and watch the units. If one sits closer to the rim, adjustment is needed. If the unit with balance screw is closer, turn screw clockwise to strengthen spring and move it out. If it is further away, turn balance screw anticlockwise. Start with half-turns, pulling the levers to ease things into place. The spring can be sensitive to quarter-turns, so move slowly.

◀ **Step 4:** Once everything else is set up, return to the brake blocks. Loosen the nut on the back of the unit so that you can manipulate the brake blocks. Push in each one until it's almost touching the rim. Each block should hit the rim at 90°, midway between the top and bottom of the rim.

◀ **Step 5:** The front of the block should be about 1mm ($^1/_{16}$ inch) closer than the back. This is called 'toeing in' and helps to prevent the brakes from squealing. People often mess about with bits of cardboard stuck behind the back of the brake block. This is just making work for yourself – look at the brake block and the rim, and set the angle of the brake block so that it's closer to the rim at the front than at the back.

◀ **Step 6:** Hold the block in place with your hand and tighten the 10mm nut gently. Once it is fairly secure, hold the eye bolt still with a 5mm Allen key and tighten the 10mm nut firmly. Try to waggle the brake block – if it moves, it's not tight enough.

Servicing calliper brake units

Follow these instructions if your calliper brakes clog with road dirt, if the brake-levers stick or if the brake doesn't return smartly when you release the brake-lever.

Always do one brake at a time – that way, you've always got a complete one to refer back to if you get stuck in the middle of reassembly. Take particular care to clean road grime away from around the return spring. There isn't much of a gap between the spring and the calliper arms, so it doesn't take much of a build-up of detritus to make everything feel sluggish.

For the full spring clean effect on tired brakes, combine this service with a new pair of blocks and a new brake cable. Once you've got all your tools out, it doesn't take much longer to do the whole lot at once, and you'll feel the difference in increased braking control straight away. Fresh brake blocks are easier on your rims, minimising wear so that they last longer.

SERVICING CALLIPER BRAKE UNITS

◄ **Step 1:** Start by cutting off the cable end on the brake cable, undoing the cable pinch bolt and pulling the brake cable and casing out of the barrel-adjuster.

◄ **Step 2:** Undo the bolt that attaches the calliper to the frame/ fork. It's either a 5mm Allen key or a 10mm nut. If you're doing both brakes at once, don't get the front and back mixed up – the pivot bolt that sticks out of the back of the front calliper and through the fork is slightly longer. Clean and inspect the fixing bolt – the 5mm Allen key type is called a sleeve nut – for cracks. Clean and inspect the bolt hole.

◀ **Step 3:** Turn the calliper over and have a look at the back surface. You don't usually get to see this side of it and it tends to collect grit. Clean it thoroughly with degreaser or bike wash and a scrubbing brush. You can see the return spring clearly from here. Get right in close and clean up all around it so it can move freely. Squeeze the brake blocks together a few times to work out stray bits and pieces of dirt or grit.

◀ **Step 4:** Turn the calliper so you can see the top and give this a good scrub, too. Again, squeeze and release the calliper and clean all the bits that squeezing it reveals. Once the whole calliper is clean, rinse off all the degreaser. Drip a little drop of oil down into the gaps between each part of the mechanism and squeeze the calliper to work the oil in. Wipe off excess – it will only collect dirt. The calliper should feel much smoother.

◀ **Step 5:** Pop a drop of oil on the calliper fixing bolt and slide the bolt back through the frame/fork. Make sure you replace any washers that sat between the calliper and the frame. These are there to stop the back of the calliper getting jammed on the frame/fork. Refit the fixing bolt.

◀ **Step 6:** Hold the calliper as shown so the wheel runs centrally between the blocks and tighten the fixing bolt firmly. Wiggle the calliper to check the fixing bolt is secure – otherwise it will work itself loose. Feed the brake cable back through the barrel-adjuster then under the pinch bolt washer. Hold the blocks against the rim, pull through any excess cable and tighten the pinch bolt firmly.

Disc brakes: powerful and reliable braking on demand

Along with suspension forks, disc brakes have been the major source of innovation in bicycles over the last few years. Once the preserve of only the priciest and flashiest machines they're now routinely specified on midrange bicycles.

There are two parts to a disc brake: the calliper, which bolts onto special mounts on your frame or fork, and the rotor (or disc), which bolts directly to your front or rear hub.

Disc brakes have two distinct advantages over rim brakes. First, they don't wear out your wheel by rubbing on the rim. Second, the hard surface of the disc rotor makes for powerful braking. Mechanical disc brakes are simpler to work on than hydraulic versions because they use standard brake levers and cables. Hydraulic disc brakes are more powerful but more expensive. Disc brakes of both types are getting lighter every year; new versions have barely any weight penalty over V-brakes. They still cost a fair chunk of extra money though.

Braking power

Braking power depends on rotor size. Large rotors, those with diameters of around 200mm (8 inches), are used for downhill racing where high-speed control is paramount. Cross-country racing, where maximum speeds are lower but weight is at a premium, tends to favour smaller rotors of 150–180mm (6–7 inch) diameter. As well as being heavier, larger discs are more prone to bending, which causes them to drag in the calliper slot.

Disc brake callipers are relatively simple to mount and need very little maintenance as long as they're kept clean. They're not in the direct firing line for anything that gets thrown up by your tyres in the same way that rim brakes are, so they will work better for longer in most conditions. People sometimes find them intimidating because they're relatively new and don't look much like anything else, but they're no more difficult to adjust than V-brakes. Bleeding is tricky, but none of the procedures are difficult. Brake fluid has to be treated with care: it will strip off your paintwork if you spill it on your frame, and stop your brakes from working if you spill it on the rotor or brake pads.

Precise adjustment takes a little care. In order to work effectively the calliper needs to be mounted so that there is a gap between the pads and the rotor on either side of the rotor. Since the rotor is bolted to the wheel, a location that cannot be changed, the gap is adjusted by moving the calliper so that it sits directly over the rotor.

Calliper adjustment

Calliper adjustment is the same whether the brake is mechanical or hydraulic. The calliper has to be bolted securely to the frame with a gap between the rotor and the pads on either side. Most hydraulic brakes work by pushing both pads onto the rim at the same time. These work best if there is an equal gap between pad and rotor on either side. Most mechanical disc brakes, and some hydraulic ones, work by pushing the outer pad onto the rotor, which flexes and gets pushed in turn onto the other pad so the rotor ends up being trapped between two pads. The system is more effective than it sounds! It works best if the gap between the rotor and the stationary pad is as small as possible to reduce the amount of flex in the rotor to a minimum.

Emerging standards

The concept of standardized component manufacture was invented for gun-making by Guillaume Deschamps for the French army. It encouraged the interchangeability between individual parts rather than the making of each gun as an individual mechanism. However, artisan gun-makers were so resistant to a process that damaged their trade that they prevented the idea from realization for more than fifty years.

Bicycles are the same. Each manufacturer has its own way of doing things, and it takes a while for any one way to be universally accepted. A standard will emerge eventually, although it is not always the best of the options available.

The two styles of calliper fitting are the Post Mount, where the bolts secure the calliper point along the frame, and the International Standard mount, where the bolts point across the frame. Shimano took a few years to enter the disc brake market, waiting sensibly until everybody was sure it was a good idea. Their predominance in the market means that since they've chosen the International Standard it has become the norm.

▲ Hope mini disc brake

Disc brakes: naming of the parts

The rotor is the proper name for the disc that gives the disc brake its essential raison d'être. As with calliper fittings, it has taken time for the manufacturers to adopt a universal fitting. They seem to be settling on the "International Standard" 6-bolt fitting with a distance of 44mm between opposite holes, as originally used by Hayes.

The rotor can get very hot, particularly on long downhills. Don't touch it until it's had a chance to cool down or you really will burn yourself. It's also easy to trap your fingers in a spinning rotor while fiddling about with the callipers. Simply don't go near the rotors when the wheel is turning. Blood will contaminate the rotor surface as will the oil from your fingers, so avoid touching the rotor surface when adjusting brakes.

Each calliper is designed to take a specific size of rotor – the diameter and thickness are crucial. A larger rotor will give you more braking power and leverage, a smaller one will be lighter. Generally, a diameter of around 160mm (6¼ inches) is good for cross country; downhill needs around 200mm (8 inches).

Thinner rotors are used for single-piston callipers, where a moving piston forces the rotor across onto a stationary pad. Thinner rotors are more flexible. They take less force to bend sideways and snap back into shape as soon as you release the brakes.

Rotors wear out eventually, although it takes a long time. Shimano says its rotors can be worn down to 0.5mm (⅟₅₀ inch) thickness, but I would change them before this. For efficient braking, the surface of the rotor must be smooth and shiny. Torn or rough surfaces mean inconsistent braking and fast pad wear. Rough surfaces are often caused by the rotor rubbing on the inside of the calliper slot, so check the alignment carefully if you have to replace a rough rotor to make sure the new one doesn't go the same way.

It's vital that the rotor bolts are fitted securely; otherwise they will rattle loose. For this reason many manufacturers fit their rotors with Torx head bolts, which are a bit like Allen keys, but have star-shaped heads instead of hexagonal ones. The Torx type is no stronger than the standard type, but the unusual tool thwarts casual tinkerers.

Newer multi-tools, like the Specialized EMT tool, come with a Torx key; otherwise they're available from car and hardware shops. Don't try to tighten the bolts with a screwdriver or Allen key because you'll just damage the bolt head.

If you ride in muddy conditions you may find that a wavy-edged rotor, like the Hope Mini, will stop the calliper from clogging. (Those people at Hope on the northern English moors have plenty of mud experience.) Having your name laser-cut in the rotor gives little mud-clearing advantage, but it does let you identify your wheels amid a pile of dismembered bike parts in the car park.

Braking efficiency

Your rotors are your braking surface – your braking efficiency will depend as much on the condition of the rotors as on the condition of your brake pads.

Cleaning discs and replacing pads should be your first priority if you're not getting enough braking power. The majority of braking problems with discs are due to dirty or oily discs or contaminated pads, rather than more glamorous bleeding issues.

Cleaning rotors

Disc brake pads absorb grease or oil from any nearby source, with an immediate effect on braking power. Keep the rotor clean. It's best to avoid touching it with your fingers as they always leave greasy marks. Some people dab grease behind the brake pads to stop them vibrating and squealing. This is also a bad idea, since the grease will, without fail, work its way onto the surface of the pads. Clean the rotors with isopropyl alcohol, which doesn't leave a dirty residue. You can get it from a chemist. Car disc brake cleaning sprays are no good. Car disc brakes run much hotter, burning off the residue the sprays leave. Bicycle disc brakes don't get hot enough. Sometimes it can be worth cleaning new disc rotors straight out of the box to help reduce burn-in time. Bicycles that get a lot of city use need their rotors cleaned more frequently.

Replacing a rotor

Get the correct size tool; if you haven't got the correct one, drop the job until you do. If you round off the bolt head, it takes all sorts of messing about to recover. Undo each bolt a little bit, maybe a couple of turns. Once you can wiggle the disc on the hub, go back around again and completely remove each bolt.

The new disc needs to be fitted facing in the right direction. Usefully, some have a rotation arrow printed on the outside. Otherwise, if the rotor has an offset arm, the arm at the top needs to point forwards.

If you reuse the old bolts, put a strip of Loctite glue on each one. New bolts come pre-glued. Fit each bolt loosely through the rotor then into the hub. Take up the slack in each bolt so the head of the bolt touches the rotor. Check the rotor fits snugly against the hub. The order in which you tighten the bolts is important. Don't simply go round in a circle, alternate across the hub as shown below.

It is of utmost importance that these bolts are tight – loose ones will rattle out very quickly, which can be messy on the trail. Check they are still tight after your first ride, and then check again every 800 kilometres (500 miles).

▼ Tighten rotor bolts alternately across the centre to hold tightening plates (A) in position

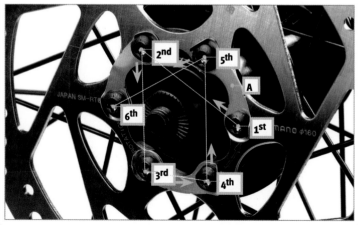

Transmission

This chapter deals with the transmission – all the parts of your bike that transfer the pedalling power to your back wheel.

The parts that make up your transmission are relatively simple, but they are exposed to the elements all the time. They also have to be kept lubricated to work efficiently. If you don't clean your transmission regularly, oil and dirt will combine to form an abrasive grinding paste that quickly eats your transmission components. Since parts mesh with each other they often have to be replaced together, so leaving your bike dirty can be a rather expensive habit.

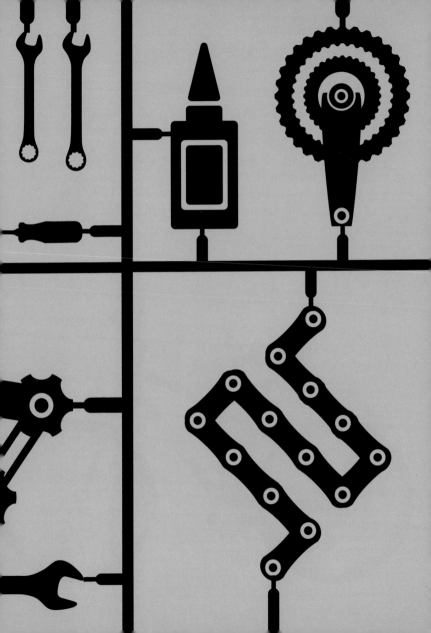

Transmission: naming the parts

You need to know what all the parts of your transmission are called before you can start fixing them; it makes going into bike shops and asking for replacement components a whole lot easier. The appearance of each mechanism may vary from bike to bike, but don't worry too much about the detail for different components: all do the same jobs regardless of what they look like. All the parts here are dealt with in more detail later in this chapter.

1) **Shifters:** It's all very well having a million gears to choose from, but you need to be able to decide which one to be in, without taking your hands off the bars. Shifters put the controls where you need them – directly under your hands. The shifter unit might be integrated with the brake-levers, making a slightly lighter combination than two separates. However, there are a couple of advantages to having separate brake-levers and gear shifters as you can adjust them independently and also replace them independently if they wear out or break.

2) **Cables and casing:** This is often neglected, but is much easier to replace than you'd imagine. A new set of cables and casing is the cheapest and most effective way to make your shifting much crisper. It makes you feel much faster, but also helps to make your transmission last as long as possible. Fresh cables means that your chain will run neatly over your sprockets and chainrings, rather than rubbing constantly and wearing itself out. The inner cable is the metal wire that runs all the way from the shifter to the derailleur. The outer casing is the plastic-covered tubing (usually black) that the cable runs through in short sections. The casing protects the cable and guides it around bends and curves.

3) **Chainset:** Your chainset is the block of gear wheels on the right-hand side of your bike, along with the pedal arm that it connects to. The individual gear wheels are called chainrings and your bike will have one, two or three of them. Road bikes normally have two: hybrids and mountain bikes three. Hub gear bikes will have a single chainring at the front. Like the rest of your transmission, chainrings will wear over time and aren't cheap to replace, but can be made to last much longer if kept clean.

4) **Cassette:** This is the cluster of sprockets in the middle of your back wheel. Derailleur geared bikes may have five, six, seven, eight, nine or 10 sprockets packed into the space between the frame and the back wheel. If the sprockets are all similar sizes, getting slightly larger as they get nearer the back wheel, your gear ratios will be very close together so that each is only slightly harder or easier than the next. Hybrids and mountain bikes tend to be fitted with cassettes that cover a wider range with larger steps between each gear.

5) **Rear derailleur:** This cunning piece of kit shifts the chain gently across your sprockets when prompted by the right-hand shifter on your handlebars, via your gear cables. These cable movements are quite small and precise, so the quality of your shifting is dependent on the condition of your cables and the fine adjustment of the cable tension. The rear derailleur also performs a handy second function – the lower of the two jockey wheels keeps the chain tensioned, so that you can use a chain long enough to go around the big sprockets, without it dragging on the ground when you shift into small sprockets.

6) **Front derailleur:** Front derailleurs are much simpler than rear derailleurs since they just perform a single function: as you operate the left-hand gear shifter, the derailleur pushes the chain from side to side across your chainset. Its simplicity as a mechanism means that it rarely needs attention and is usually quite straightforward to service, or replace. The trickiest part is usually ordering the correct replacement – there are a handful of different sizes, depending on your frame size and cable routing.

Gearing up – or down – for the smoothest possible ride

If you only had one gear, you could set the bicycle up so you had to push very hard, but each pedal stroke would make the bicycle go a long way. This is a called a high gear. Alternatively, you could set it up so you didn't have to push the pedals hard, but one pedal stroke wouldn't take you far. This is called a low gear.

Both extremes work in their own way, but your body is most efficient pedalling at a medium rate – pushing moderately hard and pedalling moderately fast – between 80 and 100 revolutions per minute. Gears were invented so that you can maintain a steady pedalling rate ("cadence" – roughly speaking, how fast your legs are going round) while the bicycle travels at different speeds.

Mountain bikes are designed to have a very wide range of gears so you can maintain an efficient cadence both when moving very slowly – for example, up a steep, rough hill at 2 mph – as well as when moving very fast – for example, plummeting downhill at 40 mph.

Small steps between the gears allow you to make subtle changes from one gear to the next, matching your pedalling speed precisely to the terrain you're cycling over. In recent years, manufacturers have steadily increased the number of gears on your cassette, giving you smaller, subtler gaps between gears, making modern bikes more responsive than their old-fashioned counterparts.

Less haste, more speed

New cyclists – along with many who've been around long enough to know better – are seduced by the idea that in order to go faster, it's imperative to force the pedals around using as much strength as possible with every stroke. With experience, it becomes plain that this only gives an illusion of speed and, in fact, serves mainly to exhaust you in the short term and wear your knees out in the long term.

Generally, you'll get where you want to go faster, feeling less exhausted, by using a lower gear: your legs spin around faster, but you don't have to press down so hard on each pedal stroke.

◀ **Shifting to a higher gear**

How gears work

Gears are easier to use than before. Shifting was a complex art, inching the lever on your frame slowly around while listening out for the clatter of the chain. It protested at being dislodged from its sprocket, then the noise died down as it meshed. Now, chains slide noiselessly from one sprocket to the next at the the touch of a button.

What's great about modern cycling is that it allows you to keep pedalling at the same rate, regardless of terrain, by varying the amount of energy it needs to turn the back wheel. Ignore this page if you can't be bothered with the maths – it makes no difference to how much you enjoy your cycling.

Imagine you no longer have a spangly 27-speed bike. Instead, you have a bike with only two chainrings at the front, which you turn by pedalling, and two sprockets on the back, which push the back wheel around when they are turned. This leaves you with a 10-tooth and 20-tooth sprocket at the back, and a 20-tooth and a 40-tooth at the front. These combinations aren't useful for cycling, but they make the maths easier.

Start with your chain running between the 40 at the front and the 10 at the back. Start with one pedal crank pointing upwards, in line with the seat-tube. Turn the cranks round exactly once. Each link of the chain gets picked up in the valley between two teeth, so that, since there are 40 teeth on the chainring, exactly 40 links of chain get pulled from the back of the bike to the front.

At the back of the bike, exactly the reverse happens. Since each link of the chain picks up one sprocket valley, pulling 40 chain links through will pull 40 sprocket valleys around. But the sprocket you're using has only 10 teeth, so will get pulled round four times (4 x 10 = 40). The sprocket is connected directly to the wheel, so in this instance turning the chainring one turn means that the

rear wheel will turn four complete turns. To measure how far this is, imagine cutting across an old tyre, to make a strip instead of a hoop, and laying it out along the ground. Measure the distance and that's how far the bike goes if you turn the wheel once. Turn the wheel four times and the bike goes four times as far.

For comparison, put the chain on the 20-tooth at the back and pop it on the 20 at the front. Now, turning the cranks around once only pulls 20 links of chain through, which in turn pulls the 20-tooth sprocket, and therefore the wheel, round exactly once. So, turning the pedals round once moves the bike forward one tyre length – a one-to-one ratio.

In the first example, the bike goes much further, but it is harder work to push the pedals around one turn. In the second example it is very easy to push the pedals round, but you don't go far. Sometimes you need to go as fast as possible, and you don't care how hard you work, so you use a combination of big chainring/small sprocket. Other times it takes all your energy simply to keep the wheels going round, so you need the easiest gear possible. Then you choose something like the last combination of small chainring/big sprocket.

Going back to the original bike you have seven, eight or nine sprockets at the back and three chainrings at the front. These allow subtle variations in how far, and easily, the bike goes when you turn the cranks. The aim is to maintain a constant cadence at a level that is most efficient for your body, over varying terrain.

Chain hygiene

A clean chain shifts neatly, whereas a dirty one shifts sluggishly and wears expensive chunks out of the drivetrain. To find out how clean your chain needs to be try reading the words stamped on the side plates. If they are legible, the chain is clean enough. If you can't read them, the chain needs your attention.

Ideally, clean your chain little and often – catching it frequently enough to only need a wipedown. This is both the laziest and the best method – take advantage of this rare combination! Leave your chain dirty for too long and you need to look at the deep-clean section later in this chapter.

After a ride lean your bike up against a wall and hold a clean, dry cloth or piece of kitchen towel around the bottom stretch of chain. Slowly pedal backward for 20 seconds, dragging the chain through the cloth. If it makes a big dirty streak, move to a clean bit of cloth and repeat. Job done. Simply do that every single time you ride and you maximize the chain's life without ever undertaking a boring major clean.

You need to lubricate the chain occasionally as well, but note that you can do as much damage by overlubricating as underlubricating. Chains need a little oil, but no more than dressing for a salad. If the chain is squeaky, you've left it too long, and the chain is gasping for lubricant. As a rough guide, oil the chain every 160km (100 miles). If the chain collects greasy, black gunk as you ride, you are over-oiling.

As above, wipe the chain with a clean cloth. Drip a drop of oil carefully onto each roller on the top surface of the bottom stretch of chain. (Drip oil is much better than spray. It goes where you want with little waste.) The important thing is to allow five minutes for the oil to soak in (have a cup of coffee), then wipe off any excess with a clean rag – drag

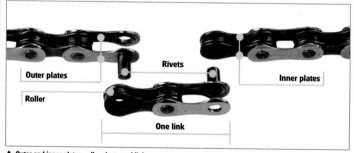

▲ Outer and inner plates, roller, rivets and link

the chain through it again. Oil is sticky. Leave it on the outside surface of the chain to pick up dirt and it makes a super grinding paste.

Cleaning your chain little and often like this ensures that it never builds up a thick layer of dirt, which means that you don't have to use harsh solvents on it.

This is well worthwhile – cleaning agents, degreasers and detergent will all soak into the internals of the chain, stripping out lubrication from the vital interface between the insides of the roller.

Each roller needs to be able to rotate freely on its rivet so that the roller can mesh neatly with the valleys between the teeth of sprockets and chainrings as you apply pressure.

Wax lubricants are an alternative to conventional oils. Several manufacturers make versions that work in similar ways. The wax sticks to your chain, protecting it from the elements but providing a layer of lubrication. The wax is not as sticky as oil, so it's less likely that dirt will adhere. But if it does, the surface of the wax will flake off, taking the dirt with it.

New layers of wax can be laid over the top since the surface should stay clean, saving you from having to clean the chain. This system means that your chain stays dry too, avoiding oily streaks on your clothes and in your home.

However, the system only really works if you start with a very clean chain – preferably a new one. A word of warning: never mix wax-based lubricants with normal ones – you end up with a sticky, slippery mess that adheres to everything except your chain.

▲ **Laziest and best: a regular wipedown**

Chain hygiene: deep clean

If your chain doesn't respond to the wipedown treatment, you must get serious. Dirty, oily chains need degreaser to clean them up.

This is strong stuff, so take care not to let it seep into bearings, where it breaks down the grease that keeps things well-lubricated. I prefer liquid degreaser, which you can apply with a brush, to the spray cans. Spray is more wasteful and harder to direct accurately.

Bike shops sell special sets of brushes, but my favourites are paint brushes. I cut off the bristles about halfway down, so what remains is firm but flexible. Keep the brushes you use for your drivetrain separate from those for frames, rims and disc rotors. Use rubber gloves to protect your hands from the degreaser.

Take your bike outside as this business always gets messy. Keep the bike upright, with the chain in the largest chainring at the front. Dip the brush into degreaser and work it into each link in the part of the chain that's wrapped around the front chainring. Do both sides, then turn the pedals around and work on the next section of chain. It takes a few minutes for the degreaser to work, so let it soak in, working around until you are back where you started.

Clean the chainrings next, front and back, picking out anything that's stuck between the chainrings or between the outer chainring and the crank arm. Clean up the derailleurs and the jockey wheels on the rear derailleur too, otherwise they dump dirt straight back onto the clean chain. Hold the back wheel upright and scrub the cassette clean. If there is compacted muck stuck between the sprockets scrape it out with a stick or skewer. Be especially careful with the degreaser at this point: keep the wheel upright to prevent it from getting into the rear hub or into the freehub.

Using a clean brush, rinse off all the degreaser with warm water. Jet-washing may be tempting but don't – ever! Dry the chain by running it through a clean rag and relubricate. Sprockets and chainrings don't need lubrication. Pop a drop of oil on the derailleur pivots, front and back.

Chain-cleaning box

A tidier option for regular cleaning is a chain-cleaning box. Fill the reservoir with degreaser, then snap the box over the lower section of chain. Pedal slowly backwards. Don't pedal too quickly or you'll splash degreaser out of the back of the box. Keep going slowly until you've used up all the degreaser. Unclip the box and take a five-minute break to give the degreaser time to break down the dirt. Rinse off with clean, warm water. Dry your chain with a clean rag and relubricate. It's worth cleaning the chain box for next time.

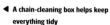

◄ **A chain-cleaning box helps keep everything tidy**

Measuring your chain for wear and tear

Your chain is under constant pressure as you pedal. A new chain arrives exactly the right size to mesh with the other components of your drivetrain.

Gradually, though, as time goes by and the miles rack up, the chain stretches. The gaps between each link grow and the chain inevitably elongates. Eventually, if you keep riding, the chain starts skipping over them instead of meshing with the teeth on the sprocket.

That's when you find yourself pushing hard on the pedals, expecting resistance. Instead of gripping, the chain slips and the pedal carrying all your weight gives way and spins like crazy, so you hurt yourself or even fall off. At this stage your chain is already worn enough to damage other components.

Joining the chain gang
If you are disciplined about measuring your chain carefully and regularly with a chain-measuring device, you can just replace the chain before it has a chance to wear the other components of your drivetrain.

This tool will tell you when you have reached this point. If you are attentive, you'll find it the cheapest option in the long term.

If you allow the chain to wear beyond this point, you will have to replace both the chain and the cassette at the same time. The old chain will have damaged the teeth on the cassette, so the new chain will be unable to mesh with it neatly.

The consequence of changing the chain without changing the sprockets is that the new chain will slip over the old sprockets, and, even if you can make it catch, the old sprockets will wear the new chain into an old chain very quickly.

If you allow the chain to wear so that it starts to slip over the cassette as you pedal, you will definitely have to change the cassette and probably some or all of the chainrings as well.

Look at the picture on this page and compare it with your chainrings – if they are starting to look like the example change them at the same time as the chain.

Note that you cannot compensate for chain stretch by taking links out of the chain to make it shorter.

The total length of the chain is not critical. It is the distance between each link that matters. If you take links out of a stretched chain, it is simply a shorter stretched chain.

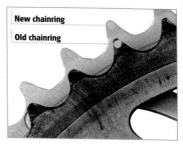

New chainring

Old chainring

▲ **Worn teeth mean the chain slips over the chainring**

MEASURING FOR WEAR

◀ **Step 1:** A chain-measuring device is the quickest and easiest way of accurately measuring your chain. The best are from Park Tools and come complete with an easy-to-read dial. Buy one today – it saves you time and money.

◀ **Step 2:** Alternatively, measure the length of 12 links. Twelve links of a new chain will measure exactly 12 inches (300mm). When it measures $12\frac{1}{8}$ inch or less, you can change the chain without changing the cassette. More than that, and you have to change the cassette as well.

◀ **Step 3:** Alternatively, put the chain on the biggest ring at the front and the smallest sprocket at the back. Hold the chain at three o'clock on the chainring and pull it outward. If the bottom jockey wheel of the rear derailleur moves, it's time for a new chain. If you can pull the chain off enough to see all or most of the tooth, you need a new cassette and probably new chainrings too.

Correct chain length and routing

It's critical to get your chain length right. If the chain is too long, it flaps about and the derailleur folds up on itself when it's in the smallest sprocket at the back and the small chainring at the front. Too short, and the chain jams when you shift into the big/big combination. These are not recommended gears, but everybody shifts into them sometimes. The right length of chain gives you the smoothest shifting and means your chain will last longer too.

The correct length chain is just long enough to wrap around the biggest sprocket at the back and the biggest chainring at the front, plus one link (a complete link is one narrow section and one wide section).

Fitting a new chain

To fit a new chain, first route it. Shift the two derailleurs so the rear one is under the biggest sprocket and the front one is over the biggest chainring. Start at the back at the lower jockey wheel and feed the end of the chain between the wheel and the lower tab. Next, feed the end between the top jockey wheel and the top tab. Route the chain around the front of the top jockey wheel, then around the back of the cassette, forward to the chainset, through the front derailleur, around a chainring, and back to meet itself. Pull the chain as tight as it will go, as in the picture below – the rear derailleur will stretch forward to accommodate it. Add one link and calculate how many links you need to remove.

If you're rejoining the chain with a split link such as a Powerlink, remember to take this into account – you only need to add an extra half-link, because the Powerlink is half a link. Including the extra link, it means that, if you have to shorten the chain to remove a twisted link, you are still left with a working chain that can reach all the gears. Join or rejoin the chain and check through the gears.

The chain should be long enough to reach around the big sprocket/big chainring combination with a little slack, but short enough so the rear derailleur doesn't fold up on itself in the small sprocket/small chainring combination. ▶

◀ **Measuring the correct chain length**

Correct chain length

To check whether the chain you have is the right length first make sure it's not too short. Step through the gears and check the chain will stretch all the way around the big sprocket at the back and the big chainring at the front. It's fine for the cage of the derailleur to be stretched forward in this gear, but make sure the chain isn't too tight – there should be enough slack to lift the middle of the lower section of chain up at least 2cm (roughly ¾ inch). Then, check it's not too long. Change gear into the smallest sprocket at the back and the smallest chainring at the front. Look at the rear derailleur cage – the lower jockey wheel will be folded right back, taking up the maximum amount of slack. Make sure it's not folded so far back that any part of the chain touches any other part. The rear derailleur folds itself up to take up the extra slack created by shifting into the small sprockets and small chainring combination with the upper (guide) jockey wheel moving forward and the lower (tension) jockey wheel moving backward and up. If the chain is too long the derailleur will fold itself up completely in the small/small combination. If the lower section of chain gets entangled with the upper jockey wheel and derailleur cage the chain will rip the rear derailleur off as you pedal. Similarly, if the chain is too short, shifting into the larger sprockets at the back while the chain is in the largest chainring will stretch the tension jockey wheel forward. If there's not enough slack, the tension in the chain can cause the back wheel to jam or it can tear off the derailleur hanger.

Why chains break and what to do about it when they do

Some people never break chains, while others seem to break them every time they ride. Chains break for different reasons, including bad luck, but sometimes these problems can be avoided.

Sometimes small rocks or pebbles are kicked up by the tyres where they get trapped between chain and cassette. As you pedal, the chain breaks across the pebble. This is just bad luck and can happen to anyone.

Changing gears while stamping hard on the pedals puts a heavy strain on a few links. The links have to move sideways across your cassette to change gear, so they're at their most vulnerable because the pressure is applied at an angle. You do have to be turning the pedals to change gear, as this is what makes the chain derail, but your chain will shift across much quicker if you can slacken off the pressure as you change. Even when going uphill try to anticipate gear changes, so that you can build up enough momentum to lift off the pressure momentarily. A well-adjusted derailleur will change from one sprocket to the next in a quarter of a revolution of the pedals, as long as it's not under too much pressure.

Your chain will be even more likely to break if the extra pressure from shifting coincides with a weak spot. Weak spots include anywhere the chain is twisted and anywhere the chain has been split and rejoined, so split your chain as little as possible.

Cassettes

Replace your chain every time you replace your cassette. Worn cassettes allow the chain to slip over the sprocket teeth, rather than to mesh securely into the valleys.

The standard fitting for attaching sprockets to the back wheel is the cassette. The cassette fits over the ratcheting mechanism, the freehub. This is bolted onto the hub with the bearing at the outboard end. The freehub allows the wheel to go round on its own without pushing the pedals, that is to freewheel.

The freehub makes a clicking noise when you freewheel. Cassettes and freehubs are made by different manufacturers, but all adhere to the standard Shimano-fitting pattern. The outer shell of the freehub is splined, a fancy way of saying it has grooves in it.

The cassette has a matching set of grooves to slide over the freehub. Everything is kept in place with a lockring that screws into the outer end of the freehub.

The first common cassettes were seven-speed. When eight-speeds were introduced, they needed a longer eight-speed freehub, but seven-speed cassettes and freehubs are not compatible with eight-speed ones. However, a nine-speed packs more sprockets into the same space, so nine-speed and eight-speed cassettes both fit onto the same freehub.

Removing the cassette

Remove the rear wheel, and take out the quick-release skewer. Note that, when you come to removing the lockring it makes a horrible noise when you loosen it. Don't worry! The lockring has a serrated surface that locks onto the serrated face of the cassette. These crunch when separated.

Lockrings that work loose can often be a source of lazy shifting – if the lockring isn't clamping the cassette securely onto the freehub body, the whole cassette will creep sideways along the freehub body when you try to change gear. This will also have the effect of causing the sprocket and freehub splines to wear prematurely.

REMOVING THE CASSETTE

◀ **Step 1:** Remove the quick-release skewer or nut, and fit the cassette-removing tool into the splines on the lockring. Make sure it fits snugly. Some tools have a hole through the middle so that you can refit the skewer or nut and hold everything in place, which is handy Alternatively, for quick-release axles, use a tool with a central rod that slides into the axle and steadies the tool.

◄ **Step 2:** Fit a chain whip around one of the sprockets on the cassette in the direction seen in this picture. This will hold the cassette still while you undo the lockring. Fit a large adjustable spanner onto the tool – you need plenty of leverage so the handle will need to be about 30cm (12 inches) long. Choose the angle so that it sticks out in the opposite direction to the chain whip.

◄ **Step 3:** With the cassette facing away, hold the chain whip in your left hand and the adjustable spanner in your right. Push down firmly on both. If you bolted the cassette lockring tool on, loosen it once the tool starts to move, to make space into which the tool can undo. Remove the lockring, then slide the cassette off the freehub by pulling it straight out from the wheel.

Refitting the cassette

Wipe clean the splines of the freehub. Slide the new or cleaned cassette onto the freehub.

Push the cassette all the way home. The outer rings are usually separate and must be correctly lined up. One of the separate rings may be narrower than the others and needs the supplied washer behind it. Grease the threads of the lockring, then screw it onto the center of the cassette. Refit the cassette-removing tool and the adjustable spanner, and tighten the lockring firmly. When the lockring is almost tight it makes an alarming crunching noise. This is normal!

◄ **Sprockets ahoy!**

Derailleurs

Derailleurs are cunning bits of gear. The way they work is simple: they take advantage of your pedalling action to move the chain smoothly from one sprocket to another. The name comes from the French for "derail" (pronounced simply "de-railer" or "de-rail-yer").

The rear derailleur hangs underneath the cassette and feeds the loose chain that's returning from the chainset back onto the cassette. This is the part of the chain that isn't under pressure – it's the top part that's doing the work as you pedal. The important part for changing gear is the guide jockey wheel, the one that sits closest to the cassette. It's also called the top jockey, even when the bicycle is upside down. The derailleur works by using the cable to move the guide jockey across the cassette. Because this part of the chain is not under pressure, the chain will follow the guide jockey and move onto a different size sprocket as it is fed onto the cassette.

The chain needs to be moving to mesh with a new sprocket, which is why you have to be pedalling to change gear. If you pedal too hard the chain will not be able to engage properly on the new sprocket, and will slip and crunch as you try to change gear.

The lower jockey wheel, also called the tension jockey, has a different function. It sits on the derailleur arm and is sprung so that it's always pushing backward. It is there because you need more chain to go around a combination of big chainring and big sprockets than for a combination of small chainring and small sprockets. The tension jockey is needed to take up the slack, otherwise the surplus chain would drag on the ground.

The derailleur is bolted on just below the rear axle. The top part stays still, but the knuckle, with the guide jockey attached, is hinged at an angle.

This means that as the guide jockey moves across, it also moves down, tracking the shape of the cassette. There is a spring across the hinge, pulling the two halves of the derailleur together. Consequently, left to its own devices, the spring will pull the derailleur so that the guide jockey runs under the smallest sprocket.

Finally, here's where you tell the derailleur what you want. The shifter on the handlebars connects to a cable, which pulls the two parts of the derailleur apart.

This moves the guide jockey across and down, and pulls the chain onto a larger sprocket. Moving the shifter the other way releases cable, allowing the spring to pull the guide jockey and chain onto a smaller sprocket.

◀ **Slave to the rhythm: the derailleur**

Indexing

In days gone by people used to be content just using the shifter to feel and listen for the right place under a particular sprocket when changing gear. Now indexed gears are universal. The shifter has notches instead of moving smoothly across its range and, if all the components are compatible and correctly adjusted, shifting one notch on the shifter pulls through enough cable to move the chain across exactly one sprocket on your cassette.

A few derailleurs are designed to work in reverse – the cable pulls the chain from the largest to the smallest sprockets and, when the cable tension is released, the spring in the rear derailleur can pull the cable back from the smallest to the largest sprocket. The Shimano Rapidrise (or Low Normal) derailleur is like this. Some people prefer it.

Adjusting your gears

Well-adjusted gears should be invisible – one click of the shifter and you should move into whatever gear you need without thinking about it. You need to lavish care on your gears to keep everything running smoothly, though. Indeed, after keeping your chain clean, the next most important thing is to keep your gears well adjusted. They don't simply work better – your entire transmission lasts longer.

Get used to adjusting your gears before you tackle any other gear work, as you have to make adjustments at the end of many procedures, especially fitting new cables or derailleurs. The rear indexing is the most important adjustment – proper tuning is not difficult, but practice makes perfect.

The most important thing to bear in mind is that your gear adjustment depends on transferring an accurate signal from your shifters to your derailleurs, so that when you take up or release a length of cable at the shifter, exactly the same amount of cable is pulled through at the derailleur. This will not happen if the cable is dirty or frayed or the casing is kinked. If you find that the adjusting instructions aren't working for you, check that cable and casing are in good condition.

◀ **Teeth that bite gently: shifting sprockets**

Adjusting the rear derailleur

Adjusting your rear derailleur can be tricky. The same problem could have one or more different – but similar – causes. Your derailleur is going to need adjusting if it's slow to shift up or down, if it changes gear all of its own accord when you're innocently cycling along, or if it rattles and clatters whenever you change gear. This is how you do it.

Adjusting your indexing: Derailleur types – standard and rapid-rise

Before you start adjusting, use the following method to check whether you have a standard derailleur or a rapid-rise derailleur. Change into one of the middle cassette sprockets. Take hold of any exposed part of the derailleur cable where it passes along the top-tube or down-tube of your bike, and pull the cable gently away from the frame. Watch the derailleur:

● If it moves towards a lower gear (larger sprocket), you have a standard derailleur – follow the instructions below.

● If the derailleur moves towards a higher gear (smaller sprocket) when you pull the cable, you have a rapid-rise derailleur – adjustment is the same in principle as for standard derailleurs, but because the spring is reversed you have to start adjustment from the other end.

Shifter types – twistshifters and triggershifters

When you adjust gears you shift repeatedly through them to test what happens. All shifters work in the same way – adjusting your indexing will be the same process whether your handlebar gear levers are twistshifters or triggershifters. Start by experimenting to see what happens to the cable when you shift. Find an exposed part of the rear derailleur cable, like you did to check whether you had a standard or rapid-rise shifter, and pull the cable gently away from

the frame with your left hand. Holding it away, use your right hand to change gear. You won't need to pedal at the same time, just operate the shifter. One movement makes the cable slacker, the other makes it tighter. Change up and down a few times so that you begin to remember which does what. For standard derailleurs, shifting so that the cable is tighter pulls the derailleur towards the wheel and onto a larger sprocket. Shifting to release the cable allows the derailleur spring to pull the derailleur away from the wheel towards a smaller sprocket. Once you are familiar with the action of your shifters, you can start indexing your gears.

People often get confused with gear indexing, mixing it up with adjusting the end-stop screw. This is also important, but it's different. The end-stop screws set the limit of the range of movement of the derailleur, stopping it from falling off either end of the sprocket. Sometimes they are set wrong and accidentally stop the chain from moving onto the sprockets at either end of the cassette.

If so, you cannot adjust your indexing properly – go to the section on end-stop screws on page 98, adjust them and then return here. Always check before you start adjusting the indexing that the chain reaches the smallest and largest sprockets, without dropping over the edge of either. To tune the indexing, pulling the cable moves the chain toward lower gears, the larger sprockets near the wheel. Releasing tension in the cable allows the derailleur spring to pull the chain outward, toward the small sprockets.

Adjusting the cable tension on standard rear derailleurs

This is possibly the single most important adjustment that you will learn to make on your bicycle and it's not difficult. There are always clear signs when you need to adjust the tension of your rear derailleur cable. If the derailleur doesn't respond to your shifter, if it shifts more than one sprocket when you click the lever, or if the chain rattles and clatters as you shift, it's time to look at your cable tension.

The important thing to remember during this procedure is to always start in the same place, with the cable tension at its slackest and the chain in the smallest sprocket. Otherwise it's easy to confuse yourself, matching up the third shifter click with the fourth sprocket, or whatever. You will either need a workstand, to keep the back wheel off the ground, or the assistance of a friend, to lift the bike up for you at the appropriate moment.

Before you begin changing the cable tension, familiarise yourself with the action of your shifter. Follow the casing that emerges from the right hand shifter to where it joins the top tube or down tube, emerging as bare cable. Hook your finger under the middle of this section of bare cable and operate your shifter – for trigger shifters, push and release one then the other. For twist shifters, rotate the shifter forwards then back. You'll feel the cable tension pull through, then release.

When the cable tension is exactly right, the chain sits exactly below each sprocket as you change gear. This maximizes chain life and stops the chain from clattering on the sprockets as you ride. Since the sprockets and shifter clicks are evenly spaced, once you have the adjustments for the two smallest sprockets the others should work automatically.

ADJUSTING REAR DERAILLEUR CABLE
You'll have to set up your bike so that you can pedal and change gear at the same time. This is one of those occasions when a workstand makes all the difference, lifting the bike off the ground so that the back wheel can turn and so that you can see everything that's going on.

The idea is to start with the chain in the smallest sprocket and the shifter in the slackest cable position, then check the gears by shifting across one sprocket at a time.

When the cable tension is exactly right, one click moves the chain one sprocket across. Increasing the tension helps the chain move to a larger sprocket; releasing tension helps it move back down to a smaller one. Big changes in cable tension must be produced by undoing the cable clamp bolt, pulling through or letting out slack and reclamping the cable. Fine-tuning – small changes in cable tension – are achieved by turning the barrel-adjuster.

Start with the shifter in high-gear position, and the chain in the smallest sprocket. Turn the pedals, and click once.

Ideally, the chain should move across to the next sprocket, and sit directly underneath it. Now move on to the steps outlined on page 97 opposite.

◀ **Step 1:** Use the barrel-adjuster to make fine adjustments. To get the barrel to move, hold it as shown with your thumb on the top of the barrel. Turning it one way tightens the cable and moves the chain away from you (A) onto larger sprockets. Turning the other way slackens the cable and allows the spring to pull the chain toward you (B) onto smaller sprockets.

◀ **Step 2:** If the derailleur doesn't move when you click the shifter the cable is far too slack. Undo the pinch bolt, pull through a little more cable by hand, tighten the pinch bolt. Start again in the smallest sprocket, clicking the shifter several times to make sure it is at the slackest position. Now increase the tension by half a turn and repeat until the chain lifts onto the second sprocket.

◀ **Step 3:** Once you can move the chain from the smallest to the second sprocket, try shifting back from the second to the smallest. You may find you have to tune the position further – try a quarter-turn at a time.

Adjusting the end-stop screw on your rear derailleur

The end-stop screws on your derailleur – also known as limit screws – prevent the derailleur from throwing the chain off either end of the cassette. This is a vital task: the end-stop prevents the chain from falling off both the largest sprocket into the gap between the cassette and the wheel and the smallest sprocket, so that it gets stuck between the cassette and the frame.

Either of these contingencies will damage your bike: cutting through the spokes where they join your rear hub or taking chunks out of your frame beside the cassette. The chain will get firmly wedged too, so the chances of you falling off and hurting yourself are quite high.

Only the heads of the end-stops screws are visible, the shafts of the screws are hidden inside the body of the derailleur. The derailleur is designed so that at either end, the tips of the end-stop screws come into contact with tabs moulded into the pivoting part of the derailleur. Screwing the end-stop screws further into the body of the derailleur means that the ends of the screws hit the tabs sooner, limiting the movement of the derailleur and preventing the derailleur from pushing the chain off either end of the cassette. If you set the end-stop screws too far in the derailleur won't be able to push the chain onto the largest or smallest sprockets.

It's easy to get confused when adjusting your rear derailleur because sometimes the same symptom can have more than one cause. For example, if you are having difficulty shifting onto the smallest sprocket, the cause could be that the "high" end-stop screw, which controls how far out the derailleur can move, is screwed too far into

the derailleur. However, too much tension in the rear derailleur cable can provoke the same response. For this reason, I find it easiest to adjust the end-stop screw when there is no tension in the rear derailleur cable. If you're fitting a new cable use these instructions to adjust the end-stop screws before you do so.

In cases where the cable is already fitted, release it from the cable stops on the frame so that it hangs loosely. To do this, first turn the pedals and change into the largest sprocket on your cassette. Stop pedalling and shift as if changing into the smallest sprocket. The chain won't be able to derail because you're not pedalling but the derailleur cable will become slack. Follow the outer casing back from the shifter to where the outer casing joins the frame at the first cable stop, and pull the casing forward toward the front of the bike. Wiggle the cable out of the slot in the cable guide. This will give you enough cable slack to adjust the end-stop screws without getting confused by cable tension issues.

Once you've finished adjusting the end-stop screws, replace the cable. To create enough slack in the cable, you'll need to push the rear derailleur toward the wheel so that it sits under the largest sprocket.

◀ **Step 1:** Start by setting the high screw. Looking at the derailleur from behind, you see the two end-stop screws, marked "H" and "L", one above the other. Normally, the higher screw adjusts the high gear, and the lower screw the low gear. The writing is often small and difficult to make out. Turn the lower screw so that the chain hangs exactly under the smallest sprocket.

◀ **Step 2:** The low end-stop screw is trickier. With the back wheel off the ground turn the pedals with your right hand. Position your left hand with first finger hooked behind the cable entry tab at the back and thumb over the forward set of pivots. Push your thumb away from you (A) while turning the pedals. Push the derailleur across, so the chain runs to the largest sprocket.

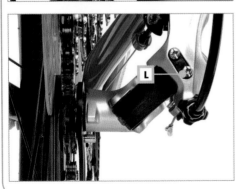

◀ **Step 3:** If you can't move the derailleur across enough to shift easily into the largest sprocket, you need to unscrew (counterclockwise) the low "L" adjustment screw. Small adjustments make a big difference, so take it easy. If the chain threatens to fall too far, wind the low screw clockwise.

Rear hanger alignment

A lot is expected of your rear derailleur. You want it to be a precise, instant-shifting piece of gear even under pressure in a dirty environment. You need to be able to rely on it in all conditions and that's why it pays to nurture it.

One of the most common problems to be routinely ignored is the alignment of the rear derailleur hanger (the part on the frame that the derailleur bolts onto). The gears are designed to work when the two jockey wheels hang vertically underneath the sprockets. This vertical alignment is the first casualty of a crash, but it's often overlooked – you get up and brush yourself off, look at your bike and, if everything looks okay, you ride away. Bad things can happen next. If you've crashed and bent your derailleur inward, the gears may still work, but everything has shipped inboard a little.

Next time you stamp uphill in a low gear, you click the lever to find a bigger sprocket, but instead you dump the chain off the inside of the rear cassette, stuffing it into the back wheel just as you haul on the pedals. Likely results include falling off and hurting yourself – and expensive damage to your back wheel.

On a less drastic level, the shifting works best when the sprockets are aligned with the jockey wheels. The chain isn't being twisted as it runs off the sprocket; and the jockey wheels move in the direction they were designed to, rather than being forced up into the sprockets as they move across the cassette, which is what happens if the hanger is bent.

Look at the derailleur from behind. This way you get the clearest view of whether or not the chain is running in one of the middle gears. The sprocket, chain and jockey wheel should make a vertical line. The most common problem occurs when the hanger is bent so that the bottom jockey wheel hangs nearer the wheel, as in the picture below.

It's not unusual for the hanger or the derailleur to be twisted rather than (or as well as!) bent. Because this is a common problem all decent aluminum frames have a replaceable hanger.

There are many different types of hanger even within a make and model; the hanger you need might depend on the year the bike was made. To make sure you get the right one, take the old one to your local bike shop for comparison. They are almost never interchangeable.

If you don't have a replaceable hanger, the frame will have to be bent back. You can do it yourself if you are careful, but if you are unsure, this is a job I recommend you take to your bike shop.

◀ Hangers need to be flat and vertical to sprockets

Improving your shifting

It's often difficult to know where to start with gear adjustment. Sluggish shifting can result from a combination of factors, both constant and intermittent. The rear derailleur, in particular, relies on everything being set up perfectly so that all the components work together.

It's also tricky to adjust gears because they behave differently under pressure. Gears that feel perfect when you're trying them out in the garage can be disappointing when you try them out for real. Occasionally, the opposite situation occurs: you can't get the gears to shift properly at all in the shop, then you go for a ride anyway and unexpectedly they feel fine.

Adjust cable tension
If you're unhappy with the shifting the most sensible place to start is with the cable tension adjustment. Click the shifters all the way into their neutral position (high gears for standard derailleurs, low for rapid-rise) and then shift over into the neighbouring sprocket. If the chain doesn't sit vertically under the sprocket or doesn't shift crisply, you have an adjustment problem – see cable tension, page 96.

Check hanger alignment
Shift into the big sprocket and look at the chain from behind the bike. The chain should make a straight vertical line down the back of the sprocket and around the jockey wheels. If the jockey wheels are tucked in towards the back wheel, you have a hanger alignment problem – see page 100.

Replace or clean cables and casing
If your cable tension and alignment are correct, but your shifting is still sluggish, your gear cable may be dirty, kinked or corroded. In particular, check the section of outer casing that

connects the rear derailleur to the frame, as it is vulnerable to getting squashed or kinked, and is near enough to the ground to pick up grit. For full suspension frames, the section of casing that links the front and back parts of the frame should also be replaced regularly.

Cables are among the least expensive parts of the bike, so changing them doesn't normally break the bank and will often make a substantial improvement to your shifting.

Clean or replace your rear derailleur
Your derailleur will work much better if it's clean and oiled. Give it a good scrub and oil it. Hold the bottom of the cage near the bottom jockey wheel and rock it gently toward and away from the wheel. Knocking, clicking or moving more than 4mm (around 1/8 inch) sideways indicates that the pivots in your derailleur are worn out.

Replace shifter
If none of these works, check that your shifter is sending crisp signals. Shift into a large sprocket, then click the shifter as if changing into a small sprocket, but without turning the pedals. This creates slack in the cable. Pull the section of casing that joins the bars to the frame forward and out of its cable stop. Slide the casing toward the back of the bike. This exposes the cable as it enters the shifter. Take hold of the cable and pull gently away from the shifter. Operate the shifter, checking that as you shift in either direction, the shifter pulls through little chunks of cable, and then releases them neatly, one at a time.

Front derailleur

The front derailleur lies directly in the firing line of all the dirt and mud that get thrown up off your back wheel, so it occasionally deserves a bit of care and attention. Cheaper front derailleurs don't last that long. I find they are the components least resistant to winter, especially if you ride on salted roads.

They get covered in whatever the roads throw up, accumulating mud that is then forced into the shifting mechanism every time you change gear. Eventually, the spring that returns the chain to the smaller chainrings can no longer cope and the derailleur stops returning when you release the cable.

▲ Front derailleurs are less complex than rear derailleurs

Front derailleur: adjusting the indexing

Like the rear derailleur, adjusting the indexing on the front derailleur is the same whatever type of handlebar shifter you have. Check what your particular shifter does by taking hold of an exposed section of cable and pulling it gently away from the frame.

Change gears in both directions to familiarize yourself with the effect that the shifters have on the cable. One of the directions or levers will loosen the cable, the other will tighten it.

Lift the back wheel off the ground for this procedure. Turn the pedals and move the front shifter so that the cable is in its slackest position. As you turn the pedals the chain should shift into the smallest chainring at the front. If it doesn't, the cable tension is too high. The barrel-adjuster for the front derailleur is up on the shifter. To loosen the cable, turn the barrel-adjuster so that the top of the barrel moves towards the front of the bike. Try a half-turn at a time to start with.

As with the rear derailleur, it is possible to get muddled between a problem with the cable tension or the end-stop screw adjustment. If you continue to adjust the cable tension, and the cable goes slack but the chain still doesn't drop into the smallest chainring when you change gear, you need to adjust the end-stop screws (A) – see pages 104–105. Adjust the end-stops, then come back here.

Once you've got the chain into the smallest ring, keep pedalling and change gear at the shifter by one complete click. The chain should climb up into the middle ring. If it doesn't, or does so sluggishly, you need to increase the tension in the cable – turn the barrel-adjuster so that the top of the barrel moves towards the back of the bike. Once the chain moves onto the middle ring, adjust the barrel until there is 1mm ($\frac{1}{16}$ inch) of clearance between the outer plate of the derailleur cage and the chain, with the chain in the smallest sprocket at the back. The chain should now shift precisely between the three rings. If it won't reach the outer or inner ring easily, you have to adjust the limit screws. They are especially likely to need adjustment if you have changed the position of the derailleur on the frame.

You may run out of barrel-adjuster – in which case you will need to turn it further out; but, as you turn, it drops out of the shifter, or you need to move it further in, but it jams against the shifter. If so, you need to make a coarse adjustment with the pinch bolt, then restart the fine adjustment. Roll the barrel most of the way back in, then undo the pinch bolt on the derailleur and pull a little cable through – start with about 3mm (around $\frac{1}{8}$ inch). Try the gears again.

Front derailleur adjustment is particularly sensitive to the position of the derailleur – if it's too high, too low or twisted, you won't be able to make it shift neatly by adjusting the cable tension. If you try the adjustment above and the derailleur still won't shift neatly, try adjusting the derailleur – follow the instructions for fitting a new one on pages 105–107. Similarly, a bent derailleur will not shift neatly. Once you've bent one, it is hard to persuade it back into the right shape. You are usually better off replacing it than trying to reshape it. It does work occasionally, but not very often.

▲ **Derailleur position is vital for crisp shifting**

Setting the end-stop screws

End-stop screws limit the movement of the derailleur so it cannot drop the chain off the outside or the inside of the chainset. If the chain won't travel far enough, even with correctly adjusted tension, check your end-stop screws.

Each end-stop screw controls the limit of the derailleur movement in only one direction. Identify the correct screw first – the marks are often printed in black on a black background. The inner screw usually adjusts the outer chain position.

SETTING END-STOP SCREWS

◀ Step 1: Start with the chain in the middle ring. Check the shifter is in the middle of the three positions. Turn the pedals and shift into high gear. The chain should lift onto the big chainring as you turn the pedals. If it won't go, you need to unwind the "high" (A) end-stop screw (marked "H" or with a wider line) on the derailleur. Unscrew the "H" screw a couple of turns and retest.

◀ Step 2: Once you've got the chain onto the big chainring, you need to make sure it won't go too far. With the chain still in the big chainring, gently roll in the "H" screw until you feel it touching the body of the derailleur – it will roll in fairly easily, then you will encounter resistance. At this point, back it off half a turn, and test again.

◀ **Step 3:** Try shifting into the smallest chainring. The chain should drop in first time. If not, back off the low adjusting screw (B). Repeat until the chain drops neatly. If it drops in straight away, set the screw so the chain can't go too far. With the chain in the smallest sprocket, wind in the "L" screw, while watching the derailleur cage – stop when you see the screw start to make the cage move.

Choosing the right type of derailleur

You need to know three bits of information to replace your derailleur with the correct type – size, pull direction and swing style. There are only three frame diameters for the front derailleur to bolt onto – 28.6, 31.8 and 34.9mm (1⅛, 1¼ and 1⅜ inch). Shimano Deore front derailleurs get lots of fitting points, since they come in one size with the correct shims for the other sizes in the packet. You also need to know the cable pull direction. For top pull derailleurs, the cable goes upwards from the derailleur, then along the top tube to your shifters. With down pull, the cable goes under the bottom bracket then up the top tube.

Check whether your derailleur is a "top swing" or a "conventional" one. Conventional types are the older design, where the cage sits lower than the frame clamp. Some full-suspension frame designs mean that this area is very crowded, so the "top swing" derailleur was introduced, taking up less space.

FITTING A FRONT DERAILLEUR

◀ **Step 1:** Shift into the little chainring to release the tension on the gear cable. Undo the cable clamp bolt, and release the cable from the derailleur. Next, undo and remove the bolt that fixes the derailleur to the frame. Fold out the hinge that clamps around your frame and pull the derailleur away from the frame.

◀ **Step 2:** The derailleur cage is still trapping the chain. Undo the small screw at the back of the derailleur cage. Ease the cage apart and slide the chain out. You will now be able to remove the old derailleur completely.

◀ **Step 3:** Undo the bolt on the back of the new derailleur cage, then slide the chain into the cage, bending it as little as possible. Support the back of the cage on the chainstay, so it doesn't get bent as you refit the cage bolt firmly.

◀ **Step 4:** Bolt the derailleur onto the frame. Start by positioning it at the same height as the old one. The correct height and angle have to be tested with the derailleur pulled out over the largest chainring. It's easiest if you test this by pulling it over by hand; things quickly get confusing if you connect the cable at this stage.

◀ **Step 5:** If it won't pull over far enough, undo the outer end-stop screw (marked with a wider line or an "H"). Pull out so that the outer cage plate is directly above the outer chainring. The front part of the cage plate should be exactly parallel to the chainring. If it isn't, loosen the fixing bolt, swing the derailleur around, and check again.

◀ **Step 6:** There should be a gap between the bottom of the outer derailleur plate and the top of the outer chainring of 1–3mm ($\frac{1}{16}$–$\frac{1}{8}$ inch). Test by pulling the derailleur out, then dropping it back and adjusting the height until it is right.

Adjusting a front derailleur

You'll need the back wheel up off the ground for this section. Turn the pedals and shift into the largest sprocket at the back.

At the front, with no cable tension, the chain should drop into the smallest chainring. If it doesn't, unwind the "L" end-stop screw. Then pull gently on the free end of the front derailleur cable and shift the shifter into the lowest gear.

Look carefully at the pinch bolt on the front derailleur and find the cable groove. Trap it in place and tighten the pinch bolt while keeping gentle pressure up on the cable.

Next, cable tension. Turn the pedals and shift into the middle gear. The chain should lift up onto the middle chainring. If it won't, or if the shift is sluggish, you need more cable tension.

Turn the barrel-adjuster on the shifter so that the top of the barrel moves backward, increasing the tension. Repeat until the chain shifts easily. Fine-tune by setting the tension, so that there is a 1mm gap between the chain and the outer plate of the front derailleur with the chain in the smallest sprocket at the back.

Fitting a new gear cable: triggershifters

Fitting a new gear cable is the easiest and cheapest way to upgrade your shifting. You'll need to arm yourself with a 5mm Allen key and a decent pair of cable cutters, as well as new cable, casing and ferrules for the ends of the sections of casing.

The procedure for changing cables is the same for front and rear shifters. Rear gear cables need changing more often because the section of cable near the back wheel gets filled with dust and mud easily, making your shifting sluggish.

For either derailleur, cut off the cable end and undo the cable clamp bolt at the derailleur. Pull the cable gently out of each section of outer casing in turn. Work all the way to the shifter, so that you end up with bare cable hanging out of the end of the shifter.

Follow the three steps on the next page to fit the new gear cable to the shifter, then route the new cable back through the outer casing to each derailleur. It's definitely worth changing the last section of outer casing on rear derailleurs every time, and any other sections that are kinked, splayed or dirty inside. If in doubt, change it! Cut each new section to length, using the old sections as a guide. Cutting the casing often squashes the lining inside – use a sharp knife to reopen the end of the lining. Fit ferrules to either end of every section of casing.

As you feed the cable through the casing, check that it slides freely. If the inner cable doesn't run smoothly through the casing now the gears won't work properly when you connect them. Replace any sections of casing that feel rough or sticky when you push cable through them. If you must use doughnuts (little protective rubber rings that stop the cable scratching the frame paint), use no more than two and make sure they're black. Feed the wire through the barrel-adjuster on the derailleur.

Check the action of the shifter by clicking through its range while pulling the cable gently away from the shifter – you should feel the shifter pulling cable through in steps. It should release in single jumps as you shift back. Replace any hatches that you removed from the shifter.

Paddle shifters

New XT and XTR shifters come as a combined unit with the downshift activated by the brake lever. The design is a cousin to the STI shifters that have become almost universal on road bikes. For cable fitting, follow the procedures for triggershifters, treating the brake lever as a gear shifter. To access the cable, remove the cover on these with a Phillips screwdriver. New cables should be lubricated as they're fitted. Any section that's going to end up inside outer casing needs a drip of oil. It doesn't need spreading about – it will gradually work its way around as you change gear. Grease is too sticky – it attracts dirt, which clogs up the outer casing. It used to be essential to put a dab of grease under the nipple as you fitted it. However, this is rarely necessary now – the nest where the nipple sits is invariably self-lubricating plastic.

FITTING A NEW GEAR CABLE

◀ **Step 1:** First pull gently on the exposed end of the cable, and shift into the gear where the cable is slackest. You may have to undo a hatch or remove a cover screw to expose the head of the cable – in this picture, a single crosshead screw is hidden between the triggers. A common variation is a pair of very small crosshead screws – take care, they will escape if you give them a chance.

◀ **Step 2:** Push the loose end of the cable gently into the shifter. If there are any slots on the barrel-adjuster, match them up with slots on the body of the shifter. As you push on the cable, the nipple will emerge from the hatch. You may need to twist it slightly to free it, or pull it free through the barrel-adjuster slots.

◀ **Step 3:** Without changing gears feed the new cable back though the shifter, reversing the procedure you used to get the old one out. Pull it firmly home so the nipple rests snugly in its nest in the shifter. Next, feed the cable through each section of outer casing in turn, with a drop of oil. Push the ferrule at the end of each section firmly into the cable stops on the frame. See page 96 to adjust cable tension.

Fitting a new gear cable: twistshifters

SRAM GripShift cables have an undeserved reputation for being difficult to fit. The very first models were a bit of a three-dimensional jigsaw puzzle, but current designs are much easier.

Precise shifting depends as much on your outer casing as inner – if the outer casing is frayed, kinked or jammed up with crud, it won't transmit a crisp signal between your shifter and your derailleur.

What you have to do is replace any sections that look unappealing as you go along. If you're cutting new sections, each one must be just long enough to reach, even when handlebars are in the turning position, but without excess. Each section must have a ferrule at either end, to prevent the ends splaying outward. You'll need a proper pair of heavy-duty cable cutters to chop outer casing – ordinary pliers won't do. Cutting the casing usually squashes the inner lining – open it back out with the point of a sharp knife before trying to push the new cable through.

You'll have to remove the old cable before you start. Cut off the cable end, undo the cable pinch bolt that clamps the cable onto the derailleur, and unthread each section of the cable back towards the shifter. Watch where it goes so that you can retrace each step with the new cable.

Cut off the old cable about 15cm (6 inches) before it enters the shifter. You'll need to shift into a particular gear to expose the head of the cable.

When you look at your gear indicators, one may be a different colour to the others or one of the numbers may have a circle drawn around it. If all the numbers look the same, shift into the highest number on the right-hand shifter (8 or 9) and into 1 on the left-hand side.

FITTING TWISTSHIFTER CABLE

◀ **Step 1:** Pull gently on the cable as it enters the shifter through the barrel-adjuster, and shift into the correct gear. Remove the escape hatch or slide it to one side, and look into the shifter. You may see the head of the nipple, or the head of a 2.5mm Allen key grub screw or a black plastic cover over half the nipple. If it's a grub screw, remove it completely.

◀ **Step 2:** If it's a plastic cover, pry it gently back with a small screwdriver. Push the exposed cable into the shifter. The nipple will emerge through the hatch. Pull the cable out of the shifter.

◀ **Step 3:** Without moving the shifter, slide the new inner cable in through the shifter. It will not feed in properly if the end of the cable is frayed, so cut off any untidiness. Pull it all the way through, make sure not to let the new cable dangle on the ground and pick up dirt. Replace the 2.5mm grub screw, if there was one, and tighten it firmly onto the nipple. Refit the escape hatch.

Other varieties of twistshifter

Some versions of twistshifters don't have a removable hatch – instead, the nipple is concealed under the edge of the rubber grip. Shift into the highest number on the right-hand shifter, or 1 on the left-hand shifter, and peel back the grip gently just below the row of numbers. You'll see the nipple – push the cable up through the barrel-adjuster; the nipple will emerge from the shifter. Feed the new cable back through without changing gear.

Removing and refitting chainsets

Why do you need to remove your chainset? There are several reasons. Either to fit a new one, to fit a new bottom bracket, to tighten your current bottom bracket in the frame, to fit new chainrings or to clean properly behind the chainset. You might also need to access suspension bushings or bolts behind there.

Removing chainsets and cranks – square taper, ISIS and Octalink

● Remove both crank bolts. Most cranks are bolted on with an 8mm Allen key. Crank bolts must be snugly fitted, so you need a long Allen key for fitting and removal – use one that is at least 200mm (8 inches) long, otherwise you won't be able to free the bolt or refit it properly at the end. Both crank bolts have conventional threads that undo anticlockwise. Check inside the crank recess for any washers and remove them.

● Look into the hole that the bolt came out of. It is one of two types, an older square taper or a newer splined taper, which will look like a notched circle. If you have an older crank extractor designed for square taper axles and a splined taper you need a special plug to pop into the end of the axle, so that the crank extractor doesn't simply disappear down inside the axle without pushing it out. If you need to get one, Shimano makes one: a tl-fc15.

● The crank extractor consists of two parts, one threaded inside the other. The outer part bolts onto the threads in the crank, the inner part then gets wound in, pushing the axle out of the crank. Before you fit the tool onto the crank, wind the inner part out so that it disappears inside the body of the tool. Hold the body of the tool steady with one wrench and wind the shaft anticlockwise.

● Clean the threads inside the crank and grease them. They are cut into the soft alloy of the crank and must be treated with respect. It's very easy to accidentally strip them with the harder threads of the crank extractor, an expensive mistake to remedy. Start the crank extractor in the crank threads by hand, then tighten home with a spanner. Don't go mad.

● Wind in the extractor shaft using the correct size of spanner. It turns quite easily until the shaft touches the end of the axle, then gets harder as it starts to push the axle out of the chainset. Once it's moving through the crank, it should slide off easily. It helps to brace the crank against the spanner so they are as parallel as possible. Keep your arms straight and use your shoulder muscles to apply the force. On the chainring side, keep your knuckles well away from the chainrings – the spanner gives suddenly, and skinned knuckles are common.

● Once you've got the cranks off, look at them. Left-hand cranks are particularly prone to damage where they fit onto the bottom bracket axle. The thread is a

The correct way to remove and refit wheels

Even if you do no maintenance on your wheels at all, it's important that you know how to take them off so that you can fix punctures. It's even more vital to be able to refit them securely – you really don't want to lose wheels as you ride along.

If you're not confident, ask your bike shop or an experienced rider to go through the procedure with you. When buying new wheels, if you're not familiar with the fitting system, ask your shop to show you how to remove and refit them.

The standard quick-release lever was designed for road-racing bicycles. It's a great system, allowing you to lock your wheels in place without tools. But the original designers of the quick-release lever had no idea what we would be doing with bicycles now. Suspension for bicycles existed already, but was a feature of butchers' and postmen's bikes and they seldom tended to use their machines for hurtling around off-road with six inches of suspension. The design has been modified along the way to make the fitting more secure – the "lawyer tabs" at the bottoms of your fork dropouts force you to undo your quick-release lever nut a few turns before you can release the wheel. This gives you a little more time to notice that something is wrong before your front wheel jumps out and plants you face first in the dirt. Similarly, the move from horizontal rear dropouts, which allow you to adjust the chain tension, was necessary to make wheels more secure. Once common on mountain bikes, these are now seen only on singlespeed-specific frames. The arrival of disc brakes has meant that hubs are subject to even stronger forces. Therefore, quick-release skewers need to be tightened securely and checked

regularly. Forks for downhill and freeride often have chunkier release mechanisms, which aren't as instant, but are more resistant to accidental release. If you find that your skewers work loose during rides, take your bike to your shop for a second opinion.

There is some disagreement about the best position for the lever. Traditionally, quick-release skewers were oriented so that the lever was on the left-hand side of the bicycle and lay along one of the stays to prevent it getting caught.

On mountain bikes it's important that the levers don't point straight forwards, because they could get caught on a branch as you ride past and flip open. I prefer to fit them on the opposite side to disc rotors, as this reduces the chances of getting burned when fixing punctures. But the shape of your forks will often dictate where the skewer can fit, especially if there are adjusting knobs or fitting bolts behind the dropout. The most important thing is to ensure that the levers are firmly fitted. A ziptie around the skewer as an extra line of defence does no harm – I especially like Shimano XT skewers for this, as they already have a handy hole in them that's the perfect size.

FITTING QUICK-RELEASE LEVERS SECURELY

◀ **Step 1:** Your skewer and hub locknut should both have deep, sharp serrations for gripping the dropout. Always use good-quality steel skewers, which should make dents in the frame where they clamp the dropouts. There should be a small steel spring on each side – both of these should point in towards the hub.

◀ **Step 2:** The lever should resist being closed. If it closes easily, flip it open again, tighten the locknut, then fold the handle closed. If the handle won't close fully, flip it open, loosen the locknut and fold closed. Once you're satisfied, flip open the lever again and twist locknut and skewer the same amount, in the same direction, so that when you close the handle it lies beside the frame or fork.

◀ **Through Axles:** Both the RockShox Maxle and Fox QR 15 systems work by threading the axle through the dropout and hub and screwing into the opposing dropout. The remaining slop is then taken up by firmly closing the quick-release lever. Each type will only work with dedicated fork and matching hub but the extra security and increased stiffness are well worthwhile.

Hubs: bearings

Bearings have been around since Roman times and appear in working drawings by Leonardo Da Vinci. His design for an early tank featured a device for enabling the gun turret to turn in different directions. He rested the upper part of the structure on a circle of wooden balls that allowed it to turn freely and support the weight (wood isn't the best bearing material, but is still used in cycle track racing rims). The modern ball bearing pioneer was Sven Wingquist, a visionary Swedish inventor who founded the SKF bearing company in 1907. The company still produces quality stainless steel bearings.

There are bearings in the centre of your wheels. They take different forms, ranging from handfuls of cheap steel balls to fancy sealed units, but they all do the same job – keep the wheel securely fixed onto your bike with no side-to-side movement, while allowing it to spin as freely as possible. Well-adjusted bearings run for years without complaint. Bearings that are too loose or too tight slow you down either way and wear out in no time, so it pays to check them regularly.

Pick up each wheel and spin it gently. It should continue rolling a couple of times on its own, even after a really gentle spin. If it slows down quickly, first check that the brake blocks or pads are not rubbing on the rim or rotor, which can have the same effect as overtight bearings. If that's the problem, go to the brakes chapter and sort them out first, then come back to bearings. If the brakes aren't the problem, then your bearing is too tight and it's slowing you down. Put the wheel down again and crouch beside the bike. Hold the rim of the back wheel where it passes between the stays (seatstays or chainstays on a hardtail, otherwise whatever lies between the main frame and the back wheel). Just pinch the rim between your thumb and finger. Hold onto the nearest bit of

frame with your other hand and rock your hands toward and away from each other, pulling the rim toward the frame then pushing it away.

The rim may flex slightly, but that's not what you're looking for. You need to check if there's a knocking feeling, or even a clicking noise, as you pull the rim back and forth. This indicates movement between the bearings and the surfaces supporting them, and means the bearings need adjustment.

Repeat with the front wheel, holding the rim where it passes through the fork and rocking gently across the bike. Again, the rim may flex slightly, but it shouldn't knock at all. The wheel should spin freely, gradually slowing down over a couple of revolutions.

Bicycle wheel bearings can be divided into two types:

◆ Cup-and-cone: Traditionally, bicycle bearings were of the cup-and-cone type – a cone-shaped nut on the axle traps a ring of bearings into a cup-shaped dip in the hub. The cone can be adjusted along the axle, making enough space for the bearings to spin but not enough for the wheel to move sideways. The cones are locked into place by wedging a locknut against each one, then tightening the cone against the locknut. The advantage here is that the parts can be serviced and adjusted with a minimum of tools.

◆ Sealed bearing hub: The modern type is called a sealed bearing hub, although the name is a bit misleading because the cup-and-cone type usually has seals too – anyway, you're liable to open up either kind and find your bearings in a mess. Instead of the cup shape, this type has a flat-bottomed round hole on each side of the hub. The bearings and the races they run on come as a unit, which is then pressed into the hole. They are trickier to fit because the bearings on each side of the wheel have to be prefectly parallel to run smoothly. The advantage here is that both the bearings and the bearing surface can be replaced when they wear. With the cup-and-cone type, the bearings and cones can be replaced, but the cup is integral to the hub and cannot be replaced cheaply.

Hub

Locknut

Seal

Cone

Bearings

Axle

Cone

Locknut

▲ Shimano Deore rear hub

Checking and adjusting cones

Wheel bearings last longest when they are properly adjusted. The purpose of your hub bearings is to allow your wheel to spin freely as you pedal, while preventing the wheel moving from side to side in the frame.

The first part is obvious – hubs that bind instead of spinning will obviously slow you down and sap your energy. But play in your bearings will slow you down as well – if your wheel can move from side to side in the frame your braking surface (the brake rotor for disc brakes, or the rim for V-brakes) gets constantly dragged against the brake pads or blocks. Loose bearings will make themselves felt when you ride as well with wheels rocking within the frame, rather than tracking your movement neatly around tight twists and turns. Your bike will feel uncertain, with small unnerving pauses, before it follows your directions.

Checking for loose bearings is the same procedure for front and back wheels. Hold onto your rim, near where it passes between the forks or the frame. Pull the rim gently towards the frame. If the bearings are loose, the rim will rock towards you – you will feel, and maybe even hear, it shifting on its bearings. It's OK if the rim flexes a little, but it shouldn't knock at all. Loose bearings need to be adjusted right away – as well as affecting your ride they will wear quickly. If the bearings are allowed to bang onto the bearing surface, instead of rolling smoothly across it, they will create pits there. Check for tight bearings at the same time. Pick up each wheel in turn and spin it. The wheel should continue to rotate freely with just the gentlest encouragement. If it slows down prematurely, check the brakes first. If the brakes aren't the problem, your bearings are too tight. Use the steps on the next page to adjust them. Front-wheel bearings are easier to adjust than rear-wheel bearings because both sides are accessible. With rear wheels, the right-hand cone and locknut are buried under the cassette.

Adjusting your bearings

Remove the wheel from the frame and remove your skewer – it just gets in the way. Spin the end of the axle between your fingers, then rock it from side to side across the wheel. If you found your bearings were too tight when you checked the wheel in your frame, the axle will feel gritty now – it may not move at all. If it felt loose in the frame, you will feel a slight rocking as you move the axle from side to side across the wheel. Since the axle runs through the centre of the wheel, you only need to work on one side of the axle to adjust both sides of the bearing. The right-hand cones on the rear wheel are concealed by the cassette, forcing you to adjust from the left side. The front can be adjusted from either side, so just follow the instructions for adjusting the back axle.

Check that the right-hand locknut is locked securely onto the axle before you start. If this side shifts about as you work on the other side, you'll not be able to set the critical distance between the two sides accurately. Hold the short stub of threaded axle that protrudes out from the middle of the locknut and try to turn the locknut. If it moves easily with your fingers, you really need to service rather than adjust the hub. Dirt and water will have been drawn into the hub as the loose cones shifted on the axle.

ADJUSTING HUBS

◀ **Step 1:** Turn the wheel so that the left-hand side of the hub faces you. Remove any black rubber seals so that you can see the locknut nearest the end of the axle and the cone behind the locknut. There may be a washer, or washers, between the cone and locknut. Slide a thin cone spanner onto the cone and hold the cone still. Use a spanner to undo the locknut one turn counterclockwise.

◀ **Step 2:** The locknut and cone on the right-hand side of the hub are locked together, clamped firmly onto the axle, so you can hold the axle still by transferring your locknut spanner onto the right locknut. Leave the cone spanner on the left hand cone and turn to adjust the bearings – clockwise to tighten, counterclockwise to loosen.

◀ **Step 3:** Holding the cone still, transfer the spanner back to the left-hand side of the hub and tighten firmly onto the cone in its new position. Check the bearing adjustment again – it can take several attempts to get the cone position right. Refit seals, skewer and back wheel. Check the bearing adjustment once you've got the wheel back in the frame – you may need to readjust.

Which tyres?

Your tyres are the only part of your bike that touches the trail or road. When you actually start to think about it, the contact patch is frighteningly small, in some cases only a couple of thumbprints. These tiny patches of rubber have to transmit the force of your pedal strokes to propel you along, steer you around corners in all kinds of loose and slippery conditions and bring you to a swift, controlled stop at the drop of a hat. So it's worth spending a little time thinking about them and paying them a bit of attention.

Puncture resistance

The single factor that's encouraged so many people to get back on their bikes in the last few years hasn't been fancy gears or radical frame materials/design – it's been an unseen strip of puncture-resistant material woven into the fabric of tyres, under the tread. Mostly used in road tyres, a puncture-resistant strip will stop the majority of nasty little sharp things worming their way through to your tube. They make the tyre slightly heavier and more expensive, but it's worth it.

Quality

A good-quality tyre will be made of stickier rubber, which will grip the road or trail better.

Pressure

Pressure is critical. The correct amount of air in your tyres is the single thing that makes a difference to how long they will last. The correct pressure is printed on the sidewall of the tyre as it's a legal requirement to include it. You'll need a pressure gauge to check the pressures at first. After a while, you get a feel for what the correct pressure feels like when you pinch the tyre, but it takes a while to learn. Many pumps come with a pressure gauge included. These are worthwhile, although the number given by

gauges on cheaper mini pumps should be treated more as an indication than an exact reading.

Tread

If you're riding off-road on trails, the shape, depth and layout of the knobbles is critical. If you are riding in muddy conditions then broad tyres, with widely spaced bars running across the rear tyre, grip where nothing else can. For harder terrain, use something with closer knobbles that has less rolling resistance. Heavier riders need a wider tyre; lighter people can get away with something narrower. But for tarmac, you generally just need to maximise the amount of rubber in contact with the road, so the smoother the better. If you're going to be riding on towpaths and the like as well as tarmac, it helps to have a smooth raised central ridge, with knobbles at the side.

▲ Smoother tyres mean more grip on tarmac

Condition

Tyres are in constant contact with the road or trail. It is inevitable that they will wear out, so inspect them regularly and often. For road tyres, take a minute every week to just go round each tyre and pick out any bits of glass or other stuff, you'll halve the number of punctures you have. It takes a while for stuff to work its way through your tyre to the tube and, if you catch it before it gets there, you'll save yourself a tube and some hassle. Slashes and holes in the surface of your tyre are an ideal shortcut for glass. Once they've begun to accumulate, replace the tyre. On mountain bikes tyres, the edges of the knobbles start to wear down. This has an impact on the level of grip the tyre can offer – no matter what tyre you choose, a fresh tyre will always grip better than a worn one.

UST tubeless tyres

UST (Universal Standard for Tubeless) mountain bike tyres do away with the inner tube and seal the tyre against the wheel rim for airtightness. No inner tube means lower rotational wheel weight (ideal for racers) and no more pinch punctures (where the inner tube pinches against the wheel rim and gets cut). Tubeless tyre set-ups are available for road bikes, too.

Wheel-truing: the science of keeping your wheels in balance

You get better at wheel-truing with practice. These instructions start you off and they can rescue you if your wheel is too buckled to ride on.

Rest the bicycle upside down, then remove the buckled wheel. Strip off the tyre and tube. This makes it easier to see what you are doing, and also releases pressure on the rim, making it easier to true accurately. Replace the wheel in the frame. Spin the wheel and look carefully at the part of the rim that passes between the brake blocks. If the wheel is too badly buckled to pass between the brake blocks, slacken off the brakes as much as possible with the barrel-adjuster on the brake lever or unit. In extreme cases, remove one or both brake blocks.

Before getting out the spoke key, have a look at the rim to confirm what you're aiming to do. Look at the part of the rim nearest you, as well as the parts of the hub you can see behind it. You will also see spokes leaving the rim and heading for the hub. There are an equal number of these, connecting alternately to the left and right sides of the hub.

Tightening a spoke that connects to the right side of the hub pulls the small portion of rim that it's connected to across to the right. Tightening a spoke that attaches to the left side of the hub pulls that part of the rim to the left. The rim is held in tension between the right spokes pulling to the right and the left spokes pulling to the left.

Slackening a left spoke allows the right spoke to pull the rim over – just as with a tug-of-war team, one team can move the central flag by pulling harder, but the same effect can result when the other team is tired and isn't pulling as hard. The aim of truing wheels is to balance the tension in all the spokes so that the lefts are pulling the same as the rights, holding the rim exactly central.

With this in mind, spin the wheel gently while watching the gap between the brake blocks and the rim. As the wheel spins, you will see that the rim moves from side to side. Imagine the centreline the rim ideally runs on, an equal distance between the brake blocks. Identify the area of the rim that has the biggest buckle.

Centre of the buckle

Look closely at the buckled area and identify the spoke at the centre of the buckle. You have to adjust the tension in this spoke to encourage the rim to sit more centrally. If the buckle pulls the rim to the right of the imaginary centreline, then spokes that go to the right-hand side of the hub must be loosened, and spokes that go to the left must be tightened.

Adjust the nipple at the centre of the rim by a half-turn. The spokes are laced alternately to the left and right sides of the hub; if one spoke goes to the left, both its neighbours must go to the right. So, once you've adjusted the spoke at the centre of the buckle by half a turn, adjust both its neighbours by a quarter-turn in the opposite direction. Spin the wheel again and look for the next biggest buckle. It may be in the

same place or somewhere else. It's better to work slowly, adjusting three spokes then checking progress by spinning the wheel.

Working out which way the nipple turns to tighten or loosen the spoke catches many people. If you get it wrong and turn the nipples the wrong way, you make each buckle worse rather than better. Eventually, if you persist, the wheel collapses. If you see things are getting worse and not better as you true, stop and think carefully about what you're doing.

Looser or tighter

When I was learning, I had to think about which way to go all the time. Eventually, I drew two circles on a piece of paper, one with a clockwise arrow that said 'looser' in the middle and one with an anticlockwise arrow saying 'tighter.'

It lived in my toolkit for ages, and every time I had to true wheels, I put it on the ground underneath the wheel. I would spin the wheel to identify the buckle, then turn it so that the area I had to work on was at the bottom, over the paper. That way, I always knew which way to turn the nipples.

After a while, your hands remember, and you don't have to think about it any more. It's a good idea to get into the habit of using the spoke key in this position, since if a spoke breaks as you turn the nipple (which happens), it hits the ground harmlessly. Don't turn the wheel so you can see the head of the nipple you're turning, as this puts your eyes and face in the firing line.

It's possible you may not get the wheel completely straight. If the wheel stops improving, stop. As long as it passes through the brake blocks, you can ride the bike somewhere to get it dealt with properly.

Fitting a new spoke

Spokes usually break as the result of a crash, but they also break from being worn out. Wheels rely on even spoke tension for strength. A broken spoke weakens the entire wheel structure.

If you have a broken spoke, remove the wheel, then the tyre, tube and rim tape, and the cassette for rear wheels. Locate the broken spoke and remove it. If it's broken near the head, pull the spoke out through the nipple hole and push the head out through the flange of the hub. If it's broken at the nipple end, push the nipple out and weave the spoke so you can pull it out of the hub.

Measure one of the other spokes to determine the length. Make sure you measure one from the same side of the same wheel as the broken one. The spoke length is measured from inside the elbow where the head curves over to the very end, which will be inside the rim, and it must be no more than 2mm (1/8 inch) different to the others.

It's vital to weave your spokes back in in the right order. Look at your hub: you'll see that alternate spokes are 'heads in' and 'heads out'. 'Heads out' spokes on the flange nearest to you appear as circles because you can only see the heads, whereas 'heads in' appear through the flange so that you can see the elbow of the spoke, which then points off toward the rim.

'Heads in' spokes are easier. Start from the far side of the hub, post the spoke across the hub and through the hole. It will now dangle on the outside of the wheel, with the head between the flanges. Pull it gently all the way through so that the head of the spoke butts up the inside of the hub. Wiggle it so that the spoke points toward the rim.

The spoke pattern repeats every four spokes, with all the 'heads in' spokes on each side of the rim radiating out in the same direction. Pick out the next similar spoke and use it as a guide. Your new spoke crosses three others on its way to the rim. The first cross is over the adjacent spoke – the 'heads in' one. These two spokes are very close so that the hub flange is between the two spokes. The new spoke passes over the next spoke it meets, but then has to be woven under the third. Line the spoke up with the empty hole in the rim, checking that the adjacent spokes in the rim head off to the opposite side.

'Heads out' is trickier. Post the new spoke a little way through the near side of the hub. Curve it gently outwards from the hub and guide the end of the new spoke out of the far side of the hub, beyond the spoke crossings. Push the head through, while maintaining the curve on the spoke with one hand.

As with 'heads in' spokes, the pattern repeats itself every four spokes. Count along three from your new spoke, in either direction, and use this one as a guide. Your new spoke crosses the adjacent spoke at the hub, passes under the next one it meets, and then has to be woven so that it passes outside the third. Line the spoke up with the empty hole in the rim, checking that the adjacent spokes in the rim head off to the opposite side of the hub.

For both types, put a drop of oil on the thread, post the nipple through from the outside of the rim and thread the nipple onto the spoke. Take up the slack with a spoke nipple, and go to page 125 to true the wheel.

What makes spokes break?

Spokes usually break on the right-hand side of back wheels. The back wheel takes more of your weight than the front, since you sit almost on top of it. Derailleur gears mean the cassette sits on the right-hand side of the hub, so the spokes on the right approach the rim at a steeper angle. They have to be tighter to keep the rim central in the frame, so they are the most vulnerable to breakage.

They are also the most awkward to replace; the cassette has to be removed to fit a standard spoke into the holes in the flange. These spokes frequently get damaged by the chain.

A badly adjusted derailleur may allow the chain to slip into the gap between cassette and spokes. If you're pedalling hard at the time (which is quite likely, since you were already in a low gear), the chain acts like a saw on your spokes, cutting through them. If you have to take the cassette off to replace a spoke behind it, inspect the others at the same time for chain damage. Replace any that have been cut or torn. It's best to swap them one at a time, so that wheel tension and shape are retained. Tighten the nipple on each replaced spoke enough to support the rim before removing and replacing the next damaged spoke. The plastic spoke protectors that sit behind your cassette are ugly, but they do prevent the chain from dropping into the gap – always replace the spoke guard after fitting new spokes.

Rim damage

Rim damage is frustrating, and often happens as a result of punctures. If the tyre deflates fast, there may not be enough time to stop before you're running on your rims. This is particularly damaging if the wheel is heavily loaded or if you're bouncing down a rocky hill. The rim sidewalls can dent, ticking constantly on the brake blocks and making the bike difficult to control during braking. Sometimes the whole rim gets a flat spot so that, as the wheel turns, and the flat spot passes between the brake blocks, the blocks rub on the tyre. Tyre sidewalls are very soft, and the brake blocks soon wear through them and the tube, causing blowouts. One of the advantages of disc brakes is that your braking isn't affected by buckled wheels in the same way, but flat spots and bent rims will still weaken the rim.

Bent sidewalls can be bent back as an emergency measure, although they will be weakened and should then be replaced as soon as is practical. A small adjustable spanner is an ideal tool; clamp it tightly onto the bulge in the rim and ease it straight. If the bulge is big, do it in several stages, working inward towards the centre from either side of the bulge.

If the rim has a flat spot, check that brakes are clear of the tyre sidewalls. If not, adjust the blocks downwards, so there is clearance even when the tyre is at its lowest relative to the blocks. It's important to check with the tyres pumped up because at higher pressures the sidewalls can bulge, throwing themselves into the path of the blocks. Once the wheel has a big flat spot, there's little you can do to correct it – if the rim bends inward more than a couple of millimetres (1/8 inch), you're looking at rebuilding the wheel with a new rim.

Tightening the spokes

It's important to take this in small steps, increasing the tension gradually and evenly, while constantly checking that the wheel remains round. The most common mistake is to crank up the tension too fast, without straightening the rim between each round of spoke tightening.

Follow steps 1–6 below for a wheel that is fairly round, true and dished. Then start again at the valve hole, and go methodically around the rim, tightening each spoke a quarter-turn. Repeat steps 3 to 6, truing the wheel more precisely. Go round again, tightening each

spoke a further turn.

Refer to a set of working wheels, so that you can compare spoke tension. Keep tightening all spokes, then correcting true, dish and hop.

TIGHTENING THE SPOKES

◀ **Step 1:** If you've just built your wheel, most spokes will be loose. Give all spokes an even amount of tension. Tighten each nipple until the spoke thread just disappears. Set wheel in the jig and spin. Pluck the spokes with a nail. To start the truing process, most need to be tight enough to hear a note. If most do, skip to next step. If not, start at the valve hole and tighten each one a quarter-turn. Repeat until the wheel has tension.

◀ **Step 2:** Once you have a degree of tension in the wheel, you can start truing it. Spin the wheel again. It probably doesn't look round at all. Your jig has an adjustable indicator – set this so that when you spin the wheel, the indicator only touches the side of the rim in one place. This is the most out-of-true section.

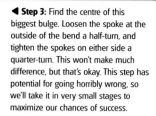

◀ **Step 3:** Find the centre of this biggest bulge. Loosen the spoke at the outside of the bend a half-turn, and tighten the spokes on either side a quarter-turn. This won't make much difference, but that's okay. This step has potential for going horribly wrong, so we'll take it in very small stages to maximize our chances of success.

◀ **Step 4:** Repeat the procedure. Spin the wheel, identify the worst bulge, loosen the spoke at the centre, tighten those at both sides, until the wheel moves from side to side no more than 10mm (3/8 inch). This can mean working repeatedly on the same area; don't worry as long as you are always attacking the biggest bulge.

◀ **Step 5:** Once you have the wheel vaguely true, spin it and check for hops. Move hop indicator on your wheel jig as close as it will go. It's easier to draw rim nearer to the hub than force it away, so concentrate on areas where rim hops outward. As with truing the wheel, work on the largest hop. When you find it, tighten the two spokes at its centre a half-turn. Repeat until the total hop in the rim is less than 3mm (3/16 inch).

◀ **Step 6:** Check the dish is correct. Turn the wheel over in the jig or in the bike without moving the indicators. If the wheel is perfectly dished, the rim sits in the same place again. If it's off to one side, it moves over in the jig. Correct by tightening all the spokes on the outer side one quarter-turn. If this is not enough, loosen all the opposite spokes a quarter-turn. Repeat until the wheel sits centrally.

Wheel words: learn the jargon

There is a proliferation of ready-built wheels on the market, but you still get the best value by attaching a hub to a hoop with a bunch of spokes yourself. If you do the weaving and tensioning yourself, you can spend the extra you save on a rim upgrade.

Your first attempt at building a wheel often takes some time, but it is a very satisfying experience. Once you've managed your first one, it gets easier every time. Don't be tempted to start with a second-hand rim and old spokes; it's much harder to true a secondhand rim, which will probably be dented and buckled, so will be frustrating since you find yourself doing the right thing without any effect.

Lacing, attaching the rim to the hub with all the spokes in the right place, comes first. This is easier than it looks. Next comes truing up the wheel so that it is round, flat and centred. This looks easier than it is and requires a fair bit of patience and care.

Front wheels are easier to start with than back ones. Back wheels have the cassette fixed on one side, which means the rim doesn't sit centrally to the hub. Therefore, the

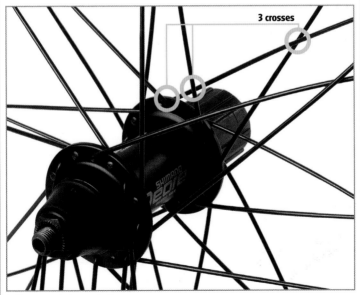

3 crosses

▲ Three-cross is the standard pattern

spokes on the cassette side have to be tighter than those on the other side. So begin your wheelbuilding career with a front wheel if you can to ease yourself into it.

Disc brakes often come with recommended spoking patterns. This is because braking applies force to only one side of the wheel, so it's important that the spokes stressed by braking are those that best support the braking force. The lacing pattern given here works best for disc brake bikes and fine for the rest, so use it for everything.

Crossing patterns

Most wheels are built 'three-cross' (3x). To see what this means, look at a wheel and follow a spoke from the hub to the rim. The spoke passes either under or over others on its way. If it crosses three other spokes, it's a standard three-cross wheel. The other common lacing pattern is 'radial', where the spokes go directly from hub to rim without crossing any others. It is also known as a zero-cross (0x) pattern.

Radial spoking is used almost exclusively for front wheels. A crossed pattern is more suitable for the back wheel; you're using the pedals to force the rear hub to turn. The spokes transfer this rotation to the rim and tyre. A crossed pattern means that the spokes leave the flange at an angle, which reduces the stress on both flange and spokes.

For both radial and crossed patterns, alternate spokes are connected to opposite flanges. This enables you to adjust the position of each section of the rim, moving it to the right by tightening spokes that connect to the right flange or loosening spokes that connect to the left flange, and moving it to the left by tightening left spokes or loosening right ones.

In crossed patterns, the spokes divide into pulling spokes and pushing spokes. The pulling spokes get tighter when you pedal and pull the hub around, dragging the rim

behind them. The pushing spokes provide a counterbalancing force, thereby keeping the wheel in its strong, round shape.

When you're braking, the opposite happens – the pushing spokes suddenly have to do all the work, with the pulling spokes supporting them.

Spoke length

Whether you're building a new wheel or replacing a broken spoke, you need to choose the correct spoke. The length needs to be exactly right – a spoke that's more than 2mm (1/8 inch) too long or too short will not fit. Minor differences in flange size (the wider part on either side of the hub, with holes through which to thread the spokes) and rim profile will affect the spoke length.

When replacing a broken spoke, check the length by measuring another on the same side of the same wheel. Spokes are measured from the very end of the threaded end to the inside of the elbow of the head end. When measuring a spoke that's laced into a wheel, you have to take the rim tape off and look into the rim from outside to estimate how much of the spoke is inside the rim.

Spokes that are too long will protrude up inside the rim, where they can puncture the tube. You can file the ends off, so that they're flush with the top of the nipple, but that's still not good enough – only the end of the nipple is threaded, so if the spoke is too long, the nipple will have to cut its own thread on the unthreaded section of the spoke. This usually just damages the nipple thread, which then won't hold spoke tension securely.

Spokes must be long enough that they're threaded most of the way onto the nipple – if the nipple is only hanging on to the spoke by the last few threads, it will pull through as soon as the spoke is stressed.

When you build a new wheel, you start from scratch. You can work out the correct length using three-dimensional trigonometry, but it's hard maths. It's easier to ask your bike shop to look it up for you – shops have tables of common hub and rim combinations, or computerized spoke-length calculating programmes. Choose a quiet time, not a busy Saturday in July. The shops are most likely to help if you buy the spokes at the same time. In order to work out the correct length, the shop needs to know the hub model, rim model, number of spokes and crossing pattern, so either take along the components you're using, or buy them at the same time.

If you're building a wheel, buy a couple of extra spokes, so that you have spares later. Don't forget to pick up nipples at the same time – they don't automatically come with spokes.

Spokes come in two types: 'rustless' – meaning they are cheap – or 'stainless'. Always build with stainless. (The savings kept from using rustless will just be spent on more spokes sooner.) Good makes include DT and Sapim.

Spoke gauge

Spokes are usually either plain gauge (the same 2mm diameter all the way along) or double-butted (2mm at the ends where they normally break, and 1.8mm in the middle to save weight). Although spokes aren't a heavy component, saving weight here is particularly significant – wheels spin around their own axles, so weight saved here makes a big difference in how easily the bike accelerates. For heavier riders, plain-gauge spokes are less stretchy, so they help keep the wheel in shape when you bounce up and down on it.

The holes in the hub flanges are only just big enough for the spokes to fit through. If the fit is very tight, the spokes are more awkward to fit, but the wheel will stay true longer. Baggy hub holes allow the spokes to shift about, wearing the holes and releasing spoke tension. The width of the flange is also important. Once again, there's a

compromise between ease of assembly and wheel longevity – if the hub flange is only slightly narrower than the elbow of the spoke, it will be tricky to ease the bend in the spoke through the hole. However the whole width of the spoke elbow will be supported by the inside of the hub hole, reducing the chance of spoke breakage. Some spokes are a smaller diameter at the threaded end. This does save a little weight, but means that you must use special 1.8mm nipples; while normal 2mm nipples will fit, they will work loose, usually over the first few miles that you use the nipples. Since a spoke gauge does vary from manufacturer to manufacturer, it makes sense to use the same make of nipple and spoke – even if they are supposed to be the same size, wheels built from mix-and–match components don't stay true as long.

Number of holes

Mountain bike wheels have mostly settled at 32 holes at the moment. The norm used to be 36, but as rims have become stronger, it's been possible to save weight by losing some spokes. Today, 28-spoke wheels are becoming more common, while 36 holes is still a good idea for heavier riders, or for those prone to trashing lots of wheels. The movement in expensive wheels is toward fewer spokes, but these are harder to build because, as you reduce the number of spokes, the tension in each becomes greater and the precision balance between the tension in each spoke becomes critical. If you've not built one before, I recommend getting good at 32- and 36-hole wheels before moving onto the fancy stuff! Road bike rims can have as few as 16 holes on the front and 20 on the rear.

Suspension

Suspension, in the form of either front forks, rear shocks, or both, is standard on mountain bikes and some road bikes, too. It is designed to iron out lumps and bumps on the trail or road. This chapter gives you an overview of some of the most common types of suspension units but to cover every type would need a whole book on its own. You'll need to use these instructions in conjunction with the owner's manual, which you can download from your manufacturer's web site. Most procedures aren't as complicated as you might think.

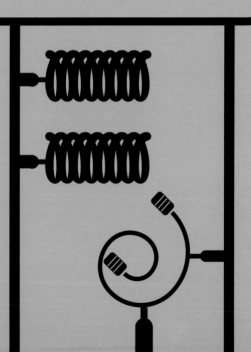

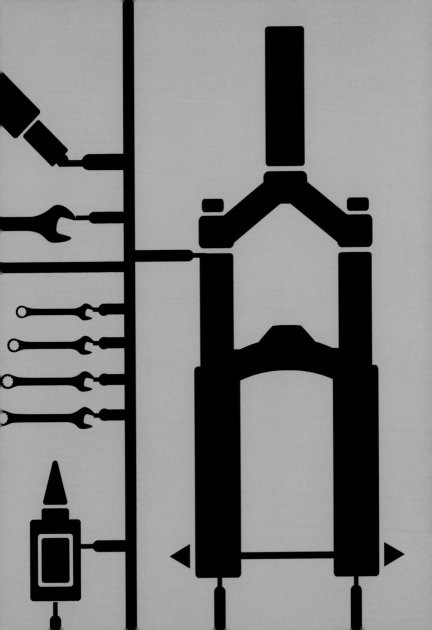

Suspension: why you need it and how it works

Suspension technology is moving very quickly. What is currently state of the art is actually more likely to be part of a great work in progress than the final form. One happy result of this is that good, reliable designs constantly get cheaper and better.

Early suspension was heavy and bounced so much when you climbed that you might as well be on a pogo stick. Full suspension is light enough to climb on now, and good design means that full suspension helps you climb by keeping the back wheel pressed down into the ground, finding whatever grip there is to help you up. Suspension isn't just for people who want to jump off roofs – it allows you to fly over rough ground without carefully picking a line as you must otherwise.

Suspension does need more care and attention than other parts of your bike. The first surprising thing is that when it's new, it needs attention straight away. When you buy a new fork, or a new bike with forks and a rear shock, you need to spend a little time adjusting it. The adjustments are very personal – nobody can set it up for you because adjustments must be done to your weight and reaction speed – and you need to take your bike somewhere safe without traffic.

Once your suspension is set up correctly, check and clean it regularly. A check and clean needs no special tools and is easy to do, but it should be done regularly. There's no harm in checking shocks after every ride, but they also need an inspection once a month.

Doing a full service on suspension forks and shocks is more advanced and often requires special tools particular to the make and model of your bike. For this, it's best to go to your bike shop or post the fork or shock off to a shock servicing specialist.

Remember to increase the frequency of servicing if you ride in sandy, salty or muddy conditions or if you cover a lot of miles.

Vital elements

Everybody claims their design is the best, but all suspension does basically the same job. A fork needs only two elements to work: a spring, which allows the wheel to move so you don't have to, and damping, which controls the speed at which the spring moves.

The spring can be a chamber of air, a coil spring, a rod of springy elastomers or a combination of all three. The spring performs the visible function – shock absorption. When you hit something, the spring gets shorter, absorbing the pressure. The stiffness of the spring controls how far it moves when you hit something – a soft spring gives a lot; a stiff spring gives a little.

The more mysterious element is damping. Damping is vital because it controls the speed of the spring action. Pogo sticks are an example of springs with no damping – if you bounce on them, they keep bouncing. This is great fun on a pogo stick but rubbish on a bike. Damping controls the speed of the spring movement.

You may be able to control the speed of the damping with external knobs, or it may be factory-set. More expensive forks allow you to control the speed of the fork compression separately from the speed at which the fork rebounds.

Front suspension

Fork servicing isn't magic. It isn't even difficult, but it does need care and patience. It often needs very specific parts, which usually have to be ordered - there must be at least a million different spare suspension part numbers out there now. Don't assume you'll get spare parts for older forks. Some companies stock a longer back catalogue than others, but if your forks are more than about three years old, you're on shaky ground. That counts from when they were first made, so if you picked them up as a cheap end-of-line model, you'll arrive in obsolete land even sooner.

Forks are generally harder to repair than to maintain – once something goes wrong or breaks, they need special parts and usually special tools as well. This is often best left to your bike shop or the fork manufacturer. If your bike shop doesn't do fork repairs, you can send your forks off to be serviced (consult your local bike shop or the Internet for a list of suppliers).

There are several designs of fork – air spring forks and coil spring forks being the main division. There isn't space here to go through a complete strip-down of every kind of fork, so I've included just a couple of examples if you're tackling this job.

The main reference text is always the owner's manual. If you don't have the one your fork came with, print a new one off the Internet. Make sure you get exactly the right year and model – even if the fork looks the same, small details change from one year to the next.

How far should you go? Use the manual for guidance – be aware that stripping down your fork further than recommended may invalidate the warranty.

Take extra care with any fork that uses an air spring. Always be sure to release all the air pressure from the fork before you take anything apart. This is easy to forget but crucial – start undoing things under pressure, and they rocket off. If they don't hit and hurt you, you'll probably lose something vital.

You should be able to service forks while they're on the bike, but you'll probably find it easier if you remove them. Either way, you'll need to be able to clamp the forks upright to add oil to the tops and to inject oil horizontally into the bottoms of the fork legs.

The most important constant maintenance for forks consists of only three things:

◆ Keep them clean, but don't jet-hose them. The most common cause of death for forks is dirt that works in between stanchions and seals, leaving scratches.

◆ Be conscious as you ride of any changes in the ride characteristic – nothing trashes forks faster than being used when something is a little loose.

◆ Ride them regularly. Forks get cantankerous if they're not ridden for a while.

There are two good reasons why people should carry out mild maintenance on their bikes more often than most do. The first is simply economic: the more expensive forks are to buy, the more expensive they are to fix. Catch a problem sooner rather than later and you save yourself money.

The second reason is safety. Suspension is good at keeping your wheels on the ground, maximizing your grip and steering, but if parts work loose and break free, you can be left with no control over your bike.

The very best time to clean your forks is just after your last ride, not just before your next one! Forks left dirty do not last as long as forks cleaned between rides. Find something wrong and you have time to fix it before going out next.

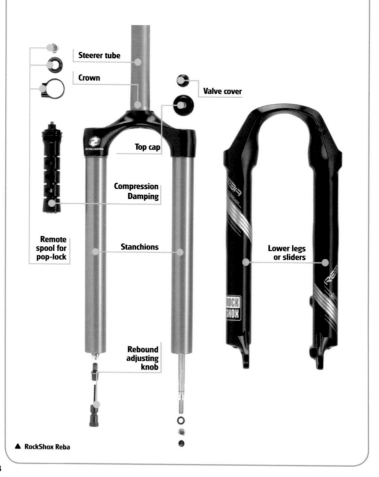

Steerer tube

Crown

Valve cover

Top cap

Compression Damping

Remote spool for pop-lock

Stanchions

Lower legs or sliders

Rebound adjusting knob

▲ RockShox Reba

Setting up your forks properly

I still get shocked by how many people spend a chunk of cash buying a new set of forks but can't find an hour to set them up properly. It's not hard and it makes an expensive fork ride like an expensive fork.

Basic forks allow you to set the preload, which you use to alter the sag. As forks get more expensive, you will also be able to adjust the rebound damping, the compression damping – the travel – and to temporarily lock out the forks to make them rigid. Different manufacturers put the controls in different places. Before you go any further, dig out your owner's manual for your fork, identify the adjustments you can make on it and locate where the adjusters are.

When setting up and tuning your forks, it's important to change just one thing at a time, so that you can see what effect you're having. If you have both front and rear suspension, set up the forks first, then set up the back end to match.

Sag

First set up the sag, which is where the fork compresses a little under your weight. The best information about how much sag your fork needs should come from your owner's manual. As a general guideline, start with 20–25 per cent of your total fork travel for cross-country forks and 30–35 per cent for downhill/freeride forks.

This is only a rough guide; your fork is designed for a specific amount of sag. Pages 140–142 guide you through setting up your fork sag.

Rebound damping

Once the sag is sorted, adjust the rebound damping. You'll need to take your bike outside and ride around for this bit. People like to lean on suspension forks, watch them spring back and nod knowledgeably, but there's no substitute for getting out and seeing how your fork reacts to being properly ridden.

Most manufacturers have a pretty good idea of a starting point for you and will recommend it in the manual. I like to set my rebound damping as fast as I can before it's so fast that the bars come back up quicker than I do. I think that's the key – to match the fork's reaction speed to yours. The faster it is, the less often it gets caught out by a series of bumps, hitting the next before recovering from the last. But it's a very personal adjustment. Your rebound damping setting affects the bike's feel when cornering – if you have too much rebound damping, the fork stays compressed as you turn, digging the wheel into the corner rather than pushing you around it.

Find a baby dropoff that you can ride over repeatedly – 10cm (4 inches) or so is about right. Set your fork to the slowest rebound damping position (i.e. maximum damping equals slowest movement), and ride over the dropoff. Reset to the fastest damping position (least damping equals fastest movement), and ride off again. You'll feel your bike react differently, with the handlebars springing straight back towards you.

Repeat the dropoff, slowing the rebound damping down a little at a time – if your adjuster has distinct clicks, go one click at a time. You're aiming to find a position where you're completely in control throughout the cycle of the fork, but with as little damping as possible.

Once you've found the right place, write down the adjustment so that you can find it again. I use a marker pen to draw a line on the fork and the knob, so that I can find the adjustment again by lining up the two marks.

Compression damping

If you have a compression damping adjustment, set this last. This adjustment affects how fast your fork compresses when it hits an obstacle. Again the right setting is tied to your reaction speed. If you set up the preload correctly and are still bottoming out, you don't have enough compression damping. If the fork doesn't respond to small obstacles, you have too much compression damping. With many forks your compression damping is

preset and cannot be adjusted. I don't think this is a great loss, I've always found the preset levels to be fine.

If you have both front and rear suspension, set up the front forks first, then set the back end to match. Set yourself a time and place where you can ride safely without looking where you're going, ideally somewhere fairly flat with a single obstacle you can ride over repeatedly without too much effort. You need to ride over the identical object a number of times to see the effect the adjustments are having.

Setting your sag

Use the steps below to measure your sag and adjust the preload to the recommended sag. Remember, this is just a starting point though.

Once you've followed the steps, ride your bike to see how it feels. If you hit something hard, you'll go all the way through the travel of the fork to the point where the top part thuds against the bottom part. This is

"bottoming out the fork". It's not a bad thing – if you don't ever hit that point during normal riding, you aren't using all the available fork travel. Play with the initial sag setting to aim to bottom out about once a ride.

SETTING YOUR SAG

◀ **Step 1:** Work out your travel. If it's written in your owner's manual, use that measurement. Manuals for air shocks often give you a recommended air pressure for your weight, but it's worth testing the actual sag you get on your bike because it depends on your position on the bike and the configuration of your shock.

◀ **Step 2:** If you don't have the manual, work travel out like this: with the fork fully extended measure the distance from the bottom of the fork crown to the top of the lower leg seal, i.e. check how much stanchion is showing.

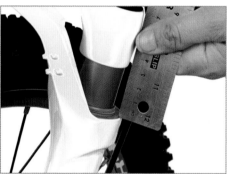

◀ **Step 3:** Release air pressure in air forks or remove coil springs in coil forks and push the fork right down as far as it will go. Measure the same distance again. Take the second number from the first. This is your total travel. Replace coil springs, reinflate air chambers.

◀ **Step 4:** Take a ziptie and loop it around one of your fork stanchions so it's fairly tight but can still be pushed up and down easily. Push it down so it sits just above the seal. Your fork may also have an O-ring installed on one of the legs for this purpose. Or markings printed on the leg.

◀ **Step 5:** Lean your bike against a wall and mount it carefully. Sit still on the bike in your normal riding position. Don't bounce up and down. Get off the bike. Your weight on the bike has compressed the forks, pushing up the ziptie. Now measure the distance between the ziptie and the top of the seal. This is the sag.

◀ **Step 6:** Adjust the air pressure or the coil-spring preload until the sag is the required proportion of the total travel.

Toolbox

- Tape measure

- Instruction book for your forks – if you haven't got the original instructions, download a replacement from the internet; make sure you get the right model and year

- Air shocks – a shock pump: almost all forks, and all shocks, use the universal Schrader fitting. However, there are a couple of anomalies which require a special valve adapter, including some Marzocchi forks. These come supplied with the fork, but you can get replacements from their distributor if you lose yours

Inspecting and maintaining your forks

Regular, careful fork maintenance will save you money – keeping your forks clean will help reduce servicing frequency. It's also a good time to inspect them, allowing you to pick up and sort out potential problems quickly.

All fork maintenance starts with a good clean. Disconnect the V-brakes and drop the wheel out of the frame, so that you can get to the forks properly. For disc brakes, push a wedge of clean cardboard between the disc pads, so that you don't accidentally pump the brake pads out of the callipers. Go through the steps below; if you find worn or broken components, it's time for a fork service. Don't ride damaged forks – they may let you down without warning.

- Start by washing the lower legs, stanchions and fork crown. Plain water is fine, although if they're really grimy, use Finish Line or other similar bike cleaners.
- As you wash the dirt off, inspect the forks carefully and methodically. Start with dropouts. Check for cracks around the joint between the fork leg and the dropout, inside and out.
- Take a look at the condition of the surfaces that your wheels clamp onto, inside and out. These grip the axle and stop the wheel popping out of the fork. The serrations on the quick-release and axle make dents in the fork – make sure that these are clean, crisp dents, rather than worn craters that indicate the wheel has been shifting about.
- Check each fork leg in turn. You're looking for splits, cracks or dents. Big dents will weaken the fork, and prevent the

stanchion from moving freely inside the lower legs. Cracks and dents both mean that it's new fork time.
- Take a look at disc and V-brake mounts. Check disc mounts for cracks and check that all calliper fixing bolts are tight.
- Check the bolts at the bottoms of the fork legs – these hold everything together, so make sure they're not working loose. Look for signs that oil has been leaking out from under the bolts.
- Clean muck out from behind the brake arch – grit has a tendency to collect here.
- Inspect the wipers that clean the stanchions as they enter the lower legs. Tears or cuts will allow grit into the wipers, where they will scour your stanchions. The tops of the wipers are usually held in place with a fine circular spring that should sit in the lip at the top of the wiper.
- Check the stanchions. If grit gets stuck in the wipers or seals, it will be dragged up and down as your fork cycles, wearing vertical grooves in the forks. These grooves in turn provide a new route in for more dirt.
- Check all the adjuster knobs. They often stick out so that you can turn them easily, but this does make them vulnerable.
- Refit the wheel and reconnect the V-brakes. Pull the front brake on and hold one of the stanchions just above the

143

lower leg. Rock the bike gently back and forth. You may be able to feel a little bit of flex in the forks, but you should not be able to feel the lower legs knocking. Lots of movement here means you need new bushings.

◆ Push down firmly on the bars, compressing the forks. They should spring back smoothly when you release the bars. If they stutter or hesitate returning, it's time for a fork service.

◆ Finally, finish off by polishing the lower legs. It makes the forks look better, which is important in itself, but also leaves a waxy finish that means dirt doesn't stick so well to the fork.

Stanchions

Wipers/seals

Lower legs

Disc mounts

Dropouts

▶ Marzocchi MX Comp

Suspension: measuring travel

Travel is the total distance your suspension unit can move. More travel means that your shock unit can absorb larger shocks, stretching out the short, sharp impacts so that you can maintain control over your bike. Longer travel allows people to do stuff on bikes that would never have been possible five years ago.

Longer travel isn't all good, though. Frames have to be beefier and heavier to maintain stiffness, as well as to withstand abuse. The shape of a long travel frame changes through the travel, making it tiring to ride long distances or to take on steep climbs. Cross-country frames with a medium amount of travel seek to find a compromise between soaking up uneven terrain, maximizing grip by keeping the rear wheel glued to the ground, and providing a comfortable, stable pedalling platform. Microtravel suspension – where the rear triangle moves 5cm (2 inches) or so – will

absorb harsh trails, adding a bit of comfort with the minimum of weight penalty.

Like front suspension, rear shocks need to be set up so that when you sit on the bike the suspension settles slightly. This is important – it means that your rear wheel can drop down into dips, as well as fold upwards to pass over lumps and obstacles in your path. This keeps you floating in a horizontal straight line, rather than climbing in and out of every irregularity on the trail, saving you energy.

Each manufacturer has their own ideas

about how much of your total travel should be taken up by this initial sag, so you'll need to consult the shock handbook or the manufacturer's website to find out their recommendations.

Since the sag is always given as a proportion of total travel, you'll need to know the travel as well before you can start setting your sag. If you don't know it already, use the steps below to measure it.

MEASURING TOTAL TRAVEL

◀ **Step 1:** Stand the bike up and measure the distance from centre to centre between the shock eyelets. This is the extended length.

◀ **Step 2:** Release the spring: for an air shock, take the valve cap off, push down the pin in the middle of the valve, pump the bike up and down a couple of times and push the pin down again to release the rest of the air. For coil shocks, back off the preload-adjuster, as far as it will go, so that the spring dangles loose.

◀ **Step 3:** Push the bike down to compress the shock and measure the distance between the eyelets again. Subtract the second measurement from the first and that's your total available travel.

Bottom brackets and headsets

These are the two main bearings that keep your pedals turning and allow you to steer your bicycle. They both get unfairly ignored too often. Bottom brackets can be replaced with a minimum of tools. Headset replacement is a job for your bike shop but regular servicing of the bearings is much simpler – since A-headsets have replaced the older threaded headsets, it can usually be done with one or two Allen keys.

Routine maintenance of the bottom bracket

The bottom bracket is the large main bearing that passes through your frame, between the cranks. Actually, it is a pair of bearings, one on each side bolted into threads cut on both sides of the frame. Like all the sealed parts of the bicycle, water and dirt will get in with enough time and abuse. This slows you down and wears out the bearings, so your bottom bracket needs regular, say annual, changing.

Back in the beginning, bottom brackets were sold in their separate parts: the axle that ran through the middle, the cups that bolted into the frame, and the bearings that sat in the gap between the two. The advantages of this system were that the gap between the bearings could be adjusted so that the bearings ran smoothly with no drag and that the parts could be regularly disassembled, cleaned, regreased, reassembled and adjusted. But we were all too lazy to do this often enough, so now almost all bottom brackets are sealed-in cartridges. They stay cleaner and, when they wear out, they have to be replaced as a unit.

Bottom brackets have a reverse thread on the right-hand side, so the cup on the chainset side of the bike has to be turned clockwise to remove it and counterclockwise to fit it. This is true of almost all bikes. The exceptions are a few fancy Italian road bikes,

which have a standard tighten-clockwise thread on both sides. These bikes serve to demonstrate why the reverse thread is necessary – bottom brackets with the Italian threading are prone to unravel under pressure from the pedals and require special attention from mechanics to stop this..

Different types of bottom bracket

Around the late 1990s, we'd finally come to settle on a standard fitting to attach cranks to bottom bracket axles when along came another improvement. History is now repeating itself with the appearance of new designs. The standard for a while was called 'square taper', which worked fine. Newer bottom brackets are splined and lighter. Your bottom bracket type must match your crank type. There is no compatibility at all between different types; you cannot exchange cranks or bottom brackets between systems.

Square taper

A square-shaped axle fits into a similar hole on the crank. Since the axle and the hole in the crank are both tapered, as you tighten the bolt on the end of the axle, you push the crank farther onto the axle, wedging it firmly in place. The idea is simple, but if the crank comes just a

little loose on the axle, it tends to loosen more, damaging the soft metal of the crank at the same time. This problem is particularly marked on the left-hand side – since the crank bolts both have a standard thread, the one on the left has a tendency to loosen as you put pressure on the pedals, whereas the right-hand one generally tightens itself. Check the bolts regularly.

Square taper

Cup

ISIS

ISIS stands for International Spline Interface Standard. This is the type of bottom bracket used by Bontrager, Race Face, Middelburn and others. There are 10 splines on each side. The chainset has matching splines. To fit the chainset to the bottom bracket, slide it over the splines and tighten until the back of the chainset butts up firmly onto the shoulder on the bottom bracket axle.

Take care lining up the second crank – the cranks fit just as easily into each of the 10 splines, so make sure your cranks point accurately in opposite directions before you tighten down the bolts.

ISIS

Crank bolts

Cup

Octalink

Shimano Octalink

This is the Shimano splined bottom bracket. It has eight splines, rather than 10 as on an ISIS bottom bracket. ISIS bottom brackets and chainsets are not compatible with Shimano ones. When refitting chainsets, always carefully clean the splines on the chainset and bottom bracket, otherwise the chainset will work itself loose as you pedal. Retighten the crank bolts after the first 50 miles.

External

The standard, pioneered by Shimano but adopted now by a raft of others, external bottom brackets use a wider, stiffer, hollow axle that's attached permanently to the chainset and bolted to the left-hand crank. The bearings are larger and sit outboard of the frame. Replacement is straightforward and they fit into the same frame threads as square- and splined- style bottom brackets.

Cup

2.5mm spacing washers

External bottom bracket

BB30 and Press Fit

First developed by Cannondale, BB30 bottom brackets have very large bearings that press directly into the frame of the bike. Shimano have their own version, the Press Fit system.

Shimano Octalink

External bottom bracket

Square taper

ISIS

Stubborn bottom brackets

Sometimes bottom brackets get wedged in hard. Usually, it means they weren't fitted with enough grease or antiseize in the first place, or that they've simply been in there too long. Try the following measures:

A good dose of release agent helps in three or four applications over a couple of days. A light spray likes WD40 will work as a basic penetrant, although you can get something tougher at your hardware or auto shop.

Once you've soaked the bottom bracket thoroughly, try using as long a lever as possible on the tool. Find a tube that fits over the end of your adjustable wrench, and use that to increase your leverage.

Creaking noises

This kind of noise from the bottom bracket area can spoil a good ride. Like all creaking sounds, investigate it right away – bicycles rarely complain unless something is loose, worn or about to snap. If your bicycle is giving you warning creaks, it's worth paying heed.

Fat-tubed aluminium bikes amplify the smallest sound. Anything with any tube fatter than you can get your hand around is, basically, a soundbox. Try these silencing measures and then test to see if the creaking has gone away. If nothing works, note that frames transmit noises strangely, so creaks can sound as if they come from somewhere else. Common causes include handlebar and stem bolts as well as rear hubs.

SORTING OUT NOISES

◀ **Step 1:** Tighten both crank bolts clockwise. They both need to be tight – you will need a long (at least 200mm [8 inch]) Allen key, not just a multi-tool. The 8mm Allen key on multi-tools is for emergencies only.

◀ **Step 2:** If that doesn't work, remove both crank bolts, grease the threads and under the heads and refit firmly.

◀ **Step 3:** Tighten both pedals. Remember that the left-hand pedal has a reverse thread – see page 183 for more details..

◀ **Step 4:** Remove both pedals, grease the threads and refit firmly. This sounds farfetched but it does the trick more often than you'd imagine. Dirt or grit on the pedal threads will also cause creaking, so clean the threads on the pedal and inside the crank.

◀ **Step 5:** Take hold of each pedal and twist it. The pedal should not move on its own axle. If it does, it could well be the source of the creak and needs stripping and servicing (see the pedals section). Spray a little light oil, like GT85, on the cleat release mechanism. Don't use chain oil – it's too sticky and will pick up dirt.

Removing and refitting the cranks: square taper and splined bottom brackets

Start on the left-hand side of the bike. Remove the Allen key bolt or 14mm Allen key that holds the crank on. Check inside the crank and remove any washers in there. Look into the hole to determine the kind of axle.

If the bike is an older or entry-level model, you will see the square end of the axle. Alternatively, you will see the round end of a splined axle.

Use the appropriate crank-extractor – splined axles are fatter, so an older crank extractor, designed for square taper cranks, cannot push out the axle. It disappears down the hole into the middle of the axle instead. Crank extractors for splined axles have a fatter head and do not fit into older square cranks. If you do have a splined axle and an older crank extractor, Shimano makes a little plug to slip into the end of your splined axle, so that the square taper crank extractor will work: a TLFC15. Sometimes one comes packaged with new chainsets.

If your crank extractor is designed for fatter, splined axles, it will not work at all with square taper axles.

REMOVING A CRANK

◀ **Step 1:** The crank bolts should be tightly fitted, so you will need a long Allen key (or 14mm socket) to undo the bolt. If you find the bolts come off without too much effort, tighten them more firmly next time!

◀ **Step 2:** Hold the handle, or the nut end of the inner part of the crank extractor and turn the outer part of the crank extractor. You will see that turning one against the other means that the inner part of the tool moves in or out of the outer part.

◀ **Step 3:** Next, back off the inner part of the tool so that its head disappears inside the outer part of the tool.

◀ **Step 4:** Thread the outer part of the tool into the threads in the crank that you've revealed by taking off the bolt. The crank is soft in comparison to the tool so take care not to cross-thread the tool and damage the crank, which will be expensive. Thread on the tool as far as it will go.

◄ **Step 5:** Start winding in the inner part of the tool. It will move easily at first, but will then meet the end of the axle and stiffen. You need to be firm with it. Once it starts moving, turning the tool gets easier as it pushes the axle out of the crank.

◄ **Step 6:** Once you've started the crank moving on the axle, the crank will come off in your hand. Pull it off the axle and remove the tool from the crank.

The crank extractor has two parts. The outer part threads onto the crank; the inner part threads through the outer part and bears on the end of the axle. As long as the outer part is firmly fitted into the crank, as you thread in the inner part, it pushes the axle off the crank. The inner part of the tool will either have an integral handle, like the Park one in the pictures above, or it will have separate flats for a spanner. Either version works fine.

If at any time the outer part of the tool starts to pull out of the chainset, stop immediately. If you continue, you will strip

the threads out of the chainset, and it will be difficult to remove the chainset without destroying it. Remove the tool from the crank and check that you've removed all bolts and washers. If there are any accidentally left in there, remove them and try again. If you can find no reason why the threads are stripping, this might be a good time to beat a retreat to your bike shop and get your mechanic to have a go.

Once you've got the left-hand crank off, repeat the procedure for the chainset side, which works exactly the same way. Once you've done whatever you need to do in the bottom bracket, you need to refit the chainset and cranks. It's worth giving the area that's behind the chainset a good clean while the rings are off, and you might as well give the chainset a good scrub with degreaser too. Rinse it off well afterward. There's no need to oil it.

Refitting the crank and chainset

The same procedure is used to fit both crank and chainset. Fit the chainset first. Before starting, clean the axle and the hole in the chainset thoroughly. Make sure there's no dirt left on the tapers or between the splines, or you will get creaking. Apply antiseize to any titanium parts.

There are two different opinions about whether the axle should be greased before you fit the cranks onto it. Proponents on both sides of the discussion are often fiercely loyal to their points of view. The advantage of greasing the axle is that the lubrication allows the crank to be pulled further onto the axle, fitting it more tightly. Those who prefer not to grease the axle say that the grease layer allows the two surfaces to move against each other, leading to potential creaking and then allowing the parts to work themselves loose. Personally, I can be convinced by either argument, but have found that it makes more difference whether the axle and crank surfaces are clean than whether they are greased. New bottom brackets often come with antiseize already applied to the right-hand axle; this should be left on.

Inspect the surface of both the axle and the holes in the cranks. Square taper axles should be flat with no pitting. The crank hole is the place you're most likely to find damage – the hole needs to be perfectly square and must fit smoothly over the axle. The most common problem is where loose cranks have rounded themselves off on the axle, smearing the shape of one or more of the corners of the square. Splined cranks will also be damaged by being ridden loose. Each spline should be crisp and clean. Replace damaged cranks immediately – they will never hold securely and will cause expensive damage to your bottom bracket axle.

Slide the chainset over the end of the axle. Line it up with the square or splined axle and push on it firmly. Grease the threads of the fixing bolts and add a dab of grease under the head of the bolt, which may otherwise creak. Fit the bolt and tighten firmly.

For the last part, line the crank up with the Allen key/socket spanner, so they are almost parallel. Hold one in each hand and stand in front of the chainset. With both arms straight, use your shoulders to tighten the crank bolts. (This uses the strength of your shoulders and reduces the chance of stabbing yourself with the chainring if you slip.)

Next, fit the crank onto the other end of the bottom bracket axle. Line it up so that it points in the opposite direction to the one on the other side. This is simple with square tapers but takes a little care with splined designs – the bike feels very strange if you fit the crank to a neighbouring spline. Tighten that crank on firmly too.

It's worth retightening all types of crank bolts after the first ride – you often find they work themselves a bit loose as they bed in. Both types of crank, square taper and splined, depend on the shape of the hole in the crank being exactly right. Riding with loose cranks stretches the shape, so the cranks will never fit firmly enough again, leaving replacement the only option. The material of the crank is softer than that of the axle, so it wears first, but if the worn crank is not replaced, it also eventually wears down the shape of the end of the bottom bracket axle.

Headsets

Your headset is the pair of bearings at the front of your bike that connects the forks to the frame. Like the bottom bracket, it's an 'out of sight, out of mind' component, frequently ignored in favour of more glamorous upgrades – but it makes a huge difference to how your bike rides. Incorrect headset adjustment and worn bearings both mean uncertain steering. A tight headset makes your steering feel heavy and wear quickly. A loose headset will rock and shudder as you brake, compromising control.

Types and styles

A Headsets are the predominant style of headset system now for almost all types of bike. They're simple to adjust and maintain, needing few special tools. A pair of bearings sit on the top and bottom of the bike's head tube. These are trapped securely in place with a pair of shaped cones. The lower one is fitted tightly to the steerer tube just below the lower bearing, whilst the upper cone sits just over the upper bearing, and can slide on the steerer tube.

To adjust the play in the bearings, the stem bolts are released so that the stem can move on the steerer tube. Then, the bolt that sits on top of the stem is adjusted. This is bolted into the top of the steerer tube, so when you tighten it, it pushes the stem, the washers below the stem, and then the top bearing cone down the steerer tube, squeezing the bearings. Once the adjustment is correct, the stem is retightened, locking the adjustment. All A Headset type systems are adjusted in a similar way, but there are a couple of variations in the way that the bearings are mounted on the frame. In a conventional set-up, a simple cup is pressed into the top and bottom of the bike's headtube, with replaceable bearings sitting

in each cup. When the bearings are worn, they can be replaced. When the cups finally wear out, they would be drifted out of the frame and a new set accurately press fitted – a job for the bike shop.

There are now a couple of variations on this theme. Integrated headsets are designed with a shoulder cut into the top and bottom of the head tube, into which a cartridge bearing is placed directly by hand. This eliminates the need to press separate cups into the frame. The shoulder is cut to a very precise size, so that the correct size and shape of cartridge fits exactly, which are designed to take the cartridge bearing. When the idea first caught on, there was the usual competing flurry of sizes, however two 'standards' quickly emerged for the cartridge size – Cane Creek (36/45), and Campagnolo (45/45). Although neater, this design does require precise machining for the cartridge seat. If this becomes damaged, the only solution may be to replace the frame.

Internal headsets are designed so that both the bearing and the headset are pressed into the head tube as a unit. Bearings can be replaced easily, but if new cups are required, again this is one for your local bike shop.

Threaded headsets

There are still a few of the older threaded headsets knocking around – you'll recognize them by the two large nuts between the stem and the frame. The lower of the two is an adjustable bearing race, used to alter the amount of space the headset bearings have to roll about in. The upper is a locknut, used to hold the correctly adjusted bearing race securely in place. The stem height is adjusted separately, with an Allen key on the top of the stem.

◀ **Step 1:** Pick the bike up by the handlebars and turn the handlebars. The bars should turn easily and smoothly, with no effort. You should not feel any notches.

◀ **Step 2:** Drop the bike back to the ground and turn the bars 90°. Hold on the front brake to stop the wheel rolling and rock the bike gently back and forth in the direction the frame (not the wheel) is pointing. The wheel might flex and the tyre yield a bit, but there should not be any knocking or play. Turning bars sideways isolates headset play, avoiding confusion with movement you may have in brake pivots or suspension.

◀ **Step 3:** Sometimes it helps to hold around the cups, above and below, while you rock the bike – you shouldn't feel any movement at all.

Aheadsets: adjusting bearings

The bearings are adjusted for no play at all, while allowing the fork and bars to rotate smoothly in the frame without resistance. Check the bearings as below; if they're tight, or there is play, adjust them. You wear your bearings really quickly if you ride them either tight or loose.

It's vital to check that your stem bolts are tight after finishing this job. Some people will tell you to leave your stem bolt slightly loose, so that in the event of a crash your stem will twist on the steerer tube rather than bending your handlebars. You should not do this. The consequences of your stem accidentally twisting on your steerer tube as you ride are far too serious and dangerous. Always tighten your stem bolts firmly. It is fine to slacken the topcap bolt off though – it's only needed for headset adjustment and can be a handy emergency bolt if something else snaps!

Checking the adjustment

A tight headset makes your steering feel heavy and wear quickly. A loose headset will make the bike rock and shudder as you brake. Either

situation will wear out your bearings quickly. To check the adjustment pick the bike up by the handlebars and turn the handlebars. The bars should turn easily and smoothly with no effort. You should not feel any notches.

Drop the bike back to the ground, and turn the bars 90 degrees, so the wheel points to one side. Hold on the front brake, to stop the wheel rolling, and rock the bike gently backwards and forwards in the direction the frame, not the wheel, is pointing. You should not feel or hear any knocking or play. Turning the bars sideways isolates headset play, avoiding confusion with any movement in your brake pivots or suspension. Sometimes it helps to hold the cups, above and below, while you rock the bike – you shouldn't feel any movement at all.

ADJUSTING AHEADSET BEARINGS

◀ **Step 1:** Loosen the stem bolt(s) so the stem can rotate easily on the steerer. Undoing the top cap makes the headset turn more easily; tightening it eliminates play. Approach the correct adjustment gradually, testing for rocking. It is easier to get the adjustment right by tightening a loose headset than by loosening a tight one.

◀ **Step 2:** If the headset is too tight, back off the topcap a few turns, hold the front brake and rock the bars gently back and forth. This frees up the headset bearings. Then gradually retighten the topcap, testing the adjustment constantly. Stop when all play is eliminated.

◀ **Step 3:** Once you have the adjustment correct, align the stem with the front wheel and firmly tighten the stem bolts. Check the stem is secure by holding the front wheel between your knees and twisting it. If you can turn it the stem bolts need to be tighter. Check the adjustment again and repeat if necessary – sometimes tightening the stem bolt shifts everything around.

Toolbox

Adjusting bearings:
- Allen keys to fit stem bolts and top cap
- Both of these are almost always a 5mm or 6mm Allen key, you may occasionally come across a 4mm Allen key fitting

Adjusting stem height:
- The same Allen keys as above, to fit your stem bolts and top cap

Servicing:
- Allen keys as above
- Tools to disconnect your brake cable, lever or disc calliper 4, 5 or 6mm Allen key
- Degreaser to clean bearing surfaces
- Quality grease – preferably waterproof
- Fresh bearings: ball bearings for headsets are generally 4mm ($\frac{5}{32}$ inch), but take old ones to a bike shop to match them up.

161

Aheadsets: stem height

If your handlebar is set at the correct height, you are more comfortable and your bike is more stable and easier to steer. You can change the height in a couple of ways.

Swapping the stem is easiest – you can change both the length of the stem and the height. Make minor changes to the height of the stem by swapping the position of the washers on it. If you take off your stem and remove a couple of washers from the steerer tube, your stem sits lower when you refit it. Replace the washers above the stem before refitting the top cap – they push the stem down the steerer tube when you tighten the top cap. You'll end up with a little stack of washers protruding above your stem.

ADJUSTING STEM HEIGHT

◀ **Step 1:** Remove the top cap. You'll need to undo the top cap bolt all the way and wiggle the cap off. This reveals that star-fanged nut inside the steerer tube. Lift off any washers that were sitting between the top cap and the stem. Check the condition of the top cap. If it's cracked or the recess where the bolt head sits is distorted, replace it.

◀ **Step 2:** Loosen the stem bolts so that the stem moves freely on the steerer tube. Pull the stem up and off – you may need to twist it a little to help it on its way. Tape the entire handlebar assembly to the top tube so that hoses and cables don't get kinked under the weight of the bars.

◀ **Step 3:** If you've hung the bike in a workstand, keep a hand on the forks so that they don't slide out of the headset. Add or remove washers from the stack under the stem. If you're adding washers, you can only add washers that came off above the stem.

◀ **Step 4:** Replace the stem, then any leftover washers – everything that came off the steerer tube should go back on. The washers are all necessary because, as you tighten the top cap, they push down onto the stem and then the bearings, adjusting the headset.

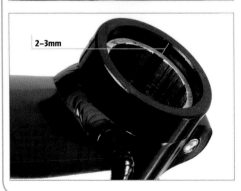

2–3mm

◀ **Step 5:** Check the height of the washer stack above the top of the steerer tube. There should be a gap of 2–3mm (around ⅛ inch). This should be a single washer, not a stack of thinner ones as individual washers have a tendency to get caught and stop you adjusting the headset properly. Add or remove washers from the top of the stack to achieve the desired 2–3mm gap.

◀ Step 6: Replace the top cap, and go to "Aheadset: adjusting bearings" on page 160. Ensure the stem bolts are securely tightened.

Headsets: regular maintenance to ensure a smooth ride

Headsets are remarkably simple to service, needing no special tools at all, just one (or two) Allen keys, degreaser or other cleaning agent and good quality grease.

Headsets, like bottom brackets, are frequently ignored, gradually deteriorating without you noticing. Regular servicing will help keep them turning smoothly and will make your bike feel more responsive. Cleaning the dirt out and replacing the grease with fresh stuff will help make the bearing surfaces last as long as possible. With the ball type, it's worth replacing the bearings at every service – new ones only cost a few dollars. Cartridge bearings are more expensive and can usually be resuscitated with care. If you're replacing them, always take the old cartridge bearings along to your bike shop to match up new ones. The size and shape are crucial.

Check carefully for pitting once you've cleaned out the headset. Even very tiny pits are a sign that your headset needs replacing.

The surface that suffers most is the crown race, the ring at the very bottom of the headset that's attached to your forks. Your bearings will quickly wear a groove in this, showing you where they run. The crown race should be completely smooth. You should be able to run a fingernail around the groove without it catching in any blemishes on the surface.

Headset hints
Before you start, remove the front wheel. It helps a lot to disconnect the front brake as well – for cable brakes, disconnect the brake cable from the lever. For hydraulic systems, either remove the brake lever from the handlebars or the brake calliper from the forks. That way, you won't damage the cable or hose when you remove the forks.

SERVICING HEADSETS

◀ **Step 1:** Undo the Allen key on the very top of the stem, the top cap bolt Remove the top cap completely, revealing the star-fanged nut inside the steerer tube. Undo the bolts that secure the stem while holding onto the forks and the stem should pull off easily.

◀ **Step 2:** Tape or tie the stem to the top tube out of the way (protect the frame paint with a cloth). Pull off any washers and set them aside. Pull the forks gently and slowly down out of the frame.

◀ **Step 3:** The fork may not want to come out. Lots of headsets have a plastic wedge that sits above the top bearing race and that sometimes gets very firmly wedged in place. Release it by sliding a small screwdriver into the gap in the plastic wedge and twist slightly to release the wedge. You could also try tapping the top of the fork with a plastic or rubber mallet.

◀ **Step 4:** Catch all pieces as they come off and note the orientation and order of bearing races and seals.

◀ **Step 5:** Once you've got the fork out, lay out all the bearing races and cups in order. Check the bearing cup at the bottom of the head tube for any bearings or seals left in there. Clean all the races carefully: the ones attached to the frame top and bottom; the loose one off the top chunk of bearings when the fork came out; and the crown race still attached to the fork.

◀ **Step 6:** Look carefully at the clean races and check for pits or rough patches. Pitted bearing races mean a new headset. This needs special tools and so is a job for your bike shop. Otherwise, clean all the bearings and seals. Grease the cups in the frame enough that the bearings sit in grease up to their middles. Cartridge bearings just need a thin smear to keep the weather out.

◀ **Step 7:** Don't grease the crown race on the fork or the loose top head race. Fit a bearing ring into the cups at either end of the head tube and replace the seals. The direction the races face is crucial, so replace them facing the same direction they were. Slide the fork back through the frame and slide the loose top race back down over the steerer tube.

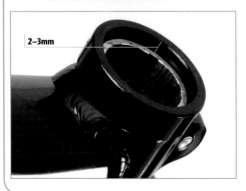

◀ **Step 8:** If it had a plastic wedge, put it next, followed by any washers or covers in the order they came off. Refit the stem and any washers from above the stem. Push the stem firmly down the steerer tube.

2–3mm

◀ **Step 9:** Make sure there's a gap of 2–3mm (around ⅛ inch) between the top of the steerer tube and the top of the stem, adding or removing washers if necessary. Refit the top cap, then adjust bearings (see page 160). Tighten the stem bolts securely, then refit your brake lever or cable and your front wheel. Check your stem is tight and facing forwards. Check front brake.

Components

When you buy a new bike, the manufacturer makes guesses about what size and shape you'll be, and chooses the "finishing kit" – handlebars, stem, seatpost and saddle – accordingly. These are personal items though and getting the right size and shape, adjusted to fit you, makes a big difference to how comfortable your ride is. Correct fit also determines how efficiently you travel. This chapter will help when you are swapping components, fitting them securely and adjusting them.

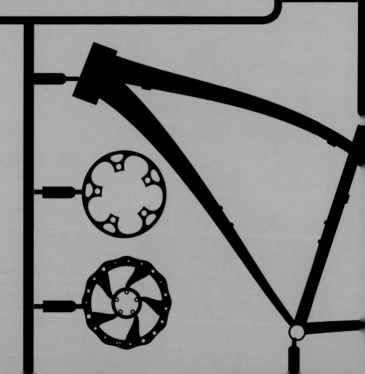

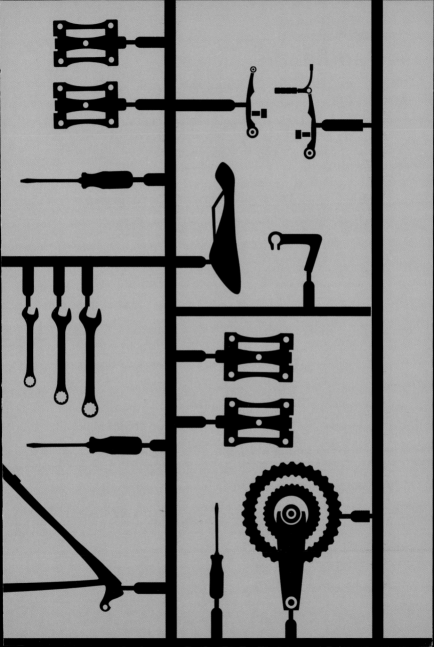

Handlebars

Renew your bars regularly, whether they show signs of cracking or not. Of all the components you use, these are the ones with a short shelf life. I like to use lightweight bars because I don't weigh much, and I like how they feel. I exchange bars every couple of years, but if I was heavier or harder on equipment, I'd replace them once or twice a year.

Removing and swapping bars whatever their shape means taking off bar tape, grips, shifters and levers. The key is remembering not to scratch the bars. It's tempting to twist and pull, leaving a spiral scour all the way along. But if you want to break a handlebar, the easiest way is to scratch it, then stress the bar repeatedly. Sound familiar?

The other damage to watch out for is crash damage – especially if you ride with bar ends. Any bending at all means they must be replaced. Both ends of the bar should be exactly the same shape and point in completely opposite directions.

Also beware of causing scratches or cracks where the stem bolts onto the handlebars. Creaking noises are a warning – always take them seriously. Sometimes the sound is caused by dirt trapped between bars and stem; sometimes it means something is about to break. Check the section on stems for help cleaning out the stem.

The standard clamp diameter is now 31.8mm – older (smaller) diameters are becoming difficult to find.

A different-shaped bar makes a surprising difference to how the bike feels. Straight, flat bars keep the front end of your body low,

spreading your weight evenly between the front and back of the bike. The aerodynamic advantage is minimal unless you ride a lot on the road, but many people find this a comfortable position.

A little extra rise, say 20mm (3⁄4 inch), makes the steering feel more precise. A slight sweep back on the bars, say 5 degrees, is easier on your wrists and shoulders. When you fit the bars, roll them until the sweep points up and back towards your shoulders. You can raise them, but don't go too far – too much height at the front end makes climbing difficult because you struggle to keep the front end of the bike on the ground.

When you refit the brake levers and shifters, spend a little time getting the angle right. I like mine set so that the brake levers are at 45 degrees to the ground, with the shifters tucked up as tight as possible underneath – but it's personal preference.

Manufacturers often save money by fitting heavier own-brand or no-brand bars on new bikes, so bars are a good place to start upgrading if you want to shave a little weight. Lightweight thin-gauge aluminium bars absorb vibrations from your bike, which helps stop your wrists from getting tired on long rides.

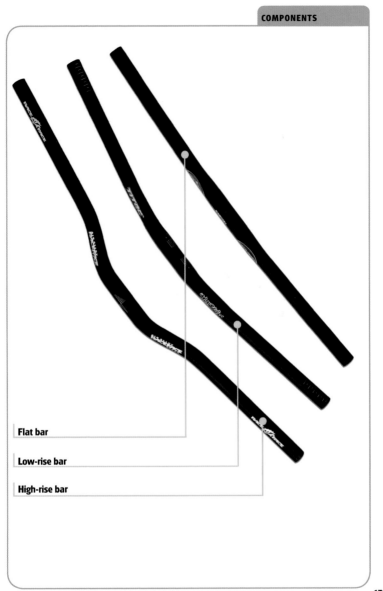

Flat bar

Low-rise bar

High-rise bar

Fitting new handlebars

Bars that have been bent in a crash need to be replaced immediately – they'll be weakened and will let you down when you least expect it. You may also be upgrading your bars for lighter or stronger ones – or for a new shape like a higher rise for more downhill control or a flatter bar to keep your weight over the front wheel when climbing.

Carbon bars are popular because they're stiff, light and strong. They need to be looked after though – a scratch on the surface will weaken them significantly. Take care when fitting and adjusting.

Next, remove the grips. Slide something underneath so that you can lift the grip up a little. It's tempting to use screwdrivers because they're the right size and handy, but it's all too easy to scratch the bars with them. Chopsticks, being made of wood, are much better. Use hairspray, spray degreaser or warm soapy water to lubricate the undergrips. Twist and pull to get the grip off.

Unbolt and remove the shifter and brake lever. Take care not to scratch the bars at all because cracks can grow from tiny scratches, especially on carbon bars. If the levers and shifters don't slide off easily, remove the fixing bolts altogether and open up the clamp very slightly with a screwdriver – just enough to slide off the levers. Don't bend the clamps, though!

You may find that cables or hydraulic hoses are too short to slide the levers off without kinking them. Don't wrestle with them: undo the bolts that hold the handlebars onto the stem and slide the handlebars along in the stem so the levers don't have to travel as far to slip off the end. Remove the handlebars.

Clean the face of the stem that the bars fit into – if dirt has worked its way in between the two parts, the bars won't clamp firmly

onto the stem and will creak as you ride. Lubricate the central part of the new bars – grease for aluminium bars, carbon prep for carbon bars.

Next, clean and grease the bolts that fix the bars onto the stem. The threads in the stem are soft and will strip easily if treated badly – this is expensive neglect because once you've stripped the threads, your only option is to replace the stem. So clean dirt out from the bolt threads and under the bolt head, then grease the threads and bolt head.

Fit the new bars loosely onto the stem, then slide the brake and gear levers onto the bars. If the cables or brake hoses are short, you may need to pass the bars from one side to the other through the stem to get the controls onto the bars without kinking the cables. Next, refit the grips. They need to be a tight fit so that they don't suddenly slide off the ends of the bars as you ride (this sounds like it would be a comic moment, but is actually disastrous and painful). You'll have to lubricate them to slide them on, but whatever you lubricate them with then needs to stick the grips to the bars. The ideal product is motorbike grip glue, but it's often hard to find. Alternatives include isopropyl alcohol, disc brake cleaner and artists' fixing spray. Don't use spray oil because it never dries properly. Set the bars in the centre of the stem, tighten the stem bolts enough to hold the bars in place, then sit on your bike to work out the

▲ Ease the clamp open slightly to avoid scratching the bars

rotations of the bar can make a big difference, so take a bit of time playing with the angle. Once you have the bar position, rotate brake levers and shifters to a comfortable angle. You need to be able to grab and operate them with as little effort as possible. Experiment with different brake-lever angles. Set the levers so that you don't have to lift your fingers too far up to get them over the lever blades.

Once you have everything in place ergonomically, go around and tighten all the fixing bolts. If your stem has a removable front face, be sure to tighten the bolts evenly so that there is an equal gap above and below the bars.

Bars are usually supplied wide, so that you can cut them down to suit your tastes. Check the manufacturer's recommendations for carbon bars before you start – if they tell you not to modify the length, follow their instructions.

most comfortable angle for the bars to sit at. If the bars are swept or curved back, a good starting place is pointing the sweep up and back towards your shoulder blades. Small

Toolbox

Tools for component upgrades
- Allen keys – 4mm, 5mm and 6mm
- Degreaser to clean interfaces and bolts
- Grease
- Chopstick to remove grips
- Grip glue or hairspray
- Cloth or paper towel for cleaning

Tools to cut bars down
- Hacksaw
- Tape measure
- File to clean off cut ends

Pedal tools: to remove and refit pedals
- Almost universally: long 15mm spanner
- For older Time pedals: long 6mm Allen key
- Grease (or antiseize for titanium axles) – otherwise your pedals will creak, and will seize into your cranks

Pedal tools: Time Alium pedals
- 6mm Allen key
- 10mm socket wrench
- New cartridge bearing – order this from your bike shop

- Degreaser to clean axle
- Grease

Pedal tools: Shimano PD-M747 pedals
- 15mm pedal spanner
- Shimano plastic pedal tool
- Shimano bearing adjustment tool or 7mm spanner and narrow 10mm spanner
- 24 2.5mm ($^3/_{32}$ inch) bearings
- Degreaser to clean bearing surfaces
- Good-quality bicycle grease

Fitting a new stem

The length and angle of the stem make a big difference to your comfort and sense of well-being, as well as to how well the bike steers.

Longer stems have the same effect as big steering wheels on cars: when they are too long the steering feels lazy, which is great for cruising but hard work for fast singletrack. Very short stems make the bike twitchy; the smallest hand movement translates into movement of your wheel, which is great for technical stuff but tiring for longer rides. The right stem length depends on your top tube length, your riding style and your body shape. Women are often more comfortable with a slightly shorter stem than men of the same size. Almost all stems are now the Ahead type. One advantage is you get two different-shaped stems in one: take it off, turn it over and refit it for a higher or lower position.

First check how the stem fits to the handlebar. It will either be a front-loader with two or four bolts or a single-bolt type. Front-loaders are the easiest to deal with: the front of the stem can be completely removed, allowing you to change or flip the stem without too much fuss. With older single-bolt stems, the handlebars can only be removed if you strip all the controls off one side of the bars.

Single bolt/quill stems

Remove the grip on one side by sliding a chopstick between grip and bar, lubricate with a squirt of light oil and twist to slide off. Loosen the bolts on the shifters and brake levers and slide them off without scratching the bars. If they're a tight fit, lever the clamps gently open with a screwdriver, without bending the clamps. The cables will often be too short to allow you to slide the controls off the end of the bar. Loosen the bolt that holds the stem to the handlebars and slide the bar sideways in the stem so that you can remove the controls without kinking the cables. Undo the bolt at the top of the stem four turns and knock it back into the stem with a rubber mallet or block of wood. This releases the wedge nut at the bottom of the stem. Twist and pull to remove it. Clean carefully inside the steerer tube. Clean the central part of the handlebars, then smear a little grease on the part that will be trapped between bars and stem. Fit the new stem to your bars. Grease the inside of the steerer tube generously and fit the bars. Make sure they're pointing directly forward, then tighten the bolt at the top of the stem firmly. Gripping your front wheel between your knees, twist the bars to check that the stem bolt is tight. If the bars rotate out of line, retighten the stem bolt. Slide the shifters and brake levers back onto your bars, then twist the grips back onto bars, lubricating with hot water if necessary. Slide the controls back up to the end of the grip and tighten the fixing bolts.

Front-loader stems

Removing

These clamp onto the handlebars with two bolts, or a bolt and a hinge. When you've undone and removed the bolt(s), you can take the front of the stem off or fold it out of the way, releasing the handlebars completely.

REFITTING

◄ **Step 1:** Clean both the stem and the handlebars where they clamp together. Once both are clean, spread a thin layer of grease or carbon prep on the part of the handlebar that's to be clamped in the stem. Grease the bolt threads with an extra dab of grease under the bolt head. Titanium bars, stems and bolts need a generous dab of copperslip.

◄ **Step 2:** It's important to do bolts up evenly. With two-bolt stems, tighten both bolts until there is an even gap between the main part and the front of the stem, then tighten each bolt one turn at a time until both are firm. With four-bolt types, tighten in a cross pattern as shown above.

◄ **Step 3:** Once the bolts are tight, check that the gap is even top and bottom and, for four-bolt types, that the gap is also even either side. This matters because the bolts will go in straight and be stronger. If one side has more gap, bolts enter the main part of the stem at an angle, stressing them and making them more likely to snap. If the front of the stem is hinged, fold over the hinge and tighten the bolt firmly.

Seatposts

Seatposts must be sized very accurately: the 30 different common sizes are sized in increments of 0.2mm. One size too big won't fit your frame; one size too small will fit but rock slightly at every pedal stroke, slowly destroying your frame. If you have your old seatpost, the right size is stamped on it. If in doubt, get your bike measured at the shop.

All seatposts have a minimum insertion line. This is usually indicated by a row of vertical lines printed or stamped near the bottom of the seatpost. The vertical lines must always be inside the frame.

If you have to lift your seatpost high enough to see the marks, you need either a longer seatpost or a bigger bike. In the unlikely event that you have no markings on your seatpost, you need a length at least 2.5 times the diameter of the post inside the frame. Seatposts that are raised too high will snap your frame.

Suspension frames with an interrupted seat tube may need a shorter seatpost, which will not bang on the shock at the bottom of its travel.

Seatpost failures

One common reason for seatpost failure is the clamp bolt shearing. Luckily, this will usually warn you by creaking as it begins to work loose. Any movement between the saddle and the seatpost needs immediate attention. Grease these bolts, both on the threads and under the head, as you fit them, and tighten snugly. If you're riding the bike and the saddle is wobbling about on the post, you'll probably have to replace the whole seatpost – the serrations on the clamp will have lost their bite and won't hold the saddle rails securely. Another issue crops up with posts that are made in two parts. Check for movement between these parts and replace the post if in doubt.

ADJUSTING SADDLE POSITION

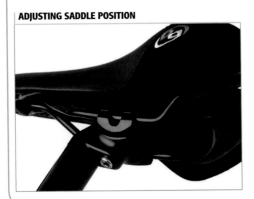

◀ **Step 1:** This is the most common type of saddle fixing. The saddle rails are clamped between two plates with a single bolt. The bottom of the lower plate is curved to match the top of the post. Loosening the bolt (6mm Allen key) allows you to slide the saddle backwards and forwards or to roll it to change the angle. Remove and regrease the fixing bolt regularly.

◀ **Step 2:** This design allows you to control the angle of the saddle precisely. To tip the saddle nose downwards, loosen the back bolt slightly and tighten the front bolt firmly, one turn at a time. To lift the nose, loosen the front bolt one turn and tighten the back bolt. To slide the saddle along on the rails, loosen both bolts equally, reposition the saddle, then retighten the bolts equally.

◀ **Step 3:** This design has two small Allen keys at the back of the clamp. Loosen both to slide the saddle rails in the clamp or to roll the clamp over the curved top of the post.

SADDLE ANGLE

◀ **Step 1:** Saddle angle is critical for a comfortable ride. Pedalling in this position, with the nose of the saddle tipped upwards, will push you off the back of the saddle, lifting the front wheel off the ground when climbing. Your thighs will also get tired with the effort of pulling your body forwards as you push down on the pedals.

◄ **Step 2:** This position can help relieve the discomfort of a saddle that doesn't suit you, but it tips you forward, towards the bars, causing wrist and shoulder pain. This position is also often a sign that your saddle is too high – try levelling it off and dropping your seatpost a few millimetres into the frame.

◄ **Step 3:** A level saddle position is always the best starting point.

Toolbox

- Allen keys – your main tool for adjusting the position of your components will almost always be the humble Allen key. Quality components deserve good-quality tools, cheap Allen keys will round off the heads of bolts, which creates plenty of frustration
- Grease – the threads of retaining bolts need a spot of grease to help tighten them firmly and stop them corroding
- Degreaser – creaking interfaces will often benefit from being stripped, cleaned and reassembled. If dirt works its way between two clamped surfaces, they'll shift about under pressure

Suspension seat posts

These have become a lot more common and are now frequently fitted to new hybrids. They used to be a bit of a gimmick to comfort people who thought they were missing out on the whole suspension revolution. In the meantime, they've quietly got better and are actually quite a good idea. They work best if you have a fairly upright riding position, which puts most of your weight onto your saddle. The suspension takes the edge off the constant jolting in and out of potholes.

Suspension seat posts often help if you get a sore back and shoulders through cycling. They are even more effective in combination with a good-quality saddle.

Getting the seat height right can take a little bit of getting used to. When you sit on the saddle it squashes the post a little bit. This is called 'sag' and is supposed to happen. It has a side effect, however, since when you get off the saddle, it pops upwards a little bit, making it seem like it's set too high. You just have to get used to lifting yourself up a little higher to get up onto the saddle. The alternative is to set it to your normal height, so that it's easier to get on to but, once you're aboard, the slight sag means you're sitting too low down so your legs never get to have a proper stretch.

The standard pattern seat post – there is remarkably little variation in design – works by trapping a spring between two telescoping parts of post. The bottom part of the post that fits into the frame looks normal. The top section of the post is narrower and slides into the bottom part. This top part may be covered with a flexible rubber boot to keep the dirt out. The spring lives inside between the two parts and may either be a long metal coil spring or an elastomer rod.

Before you ride, the sag in the seat post

ADJUSTING SAG FOR SUSPENSION SEAT POSTS

◄ **Step 1:** Lean the bike against a wall and measure from the top of the seat post - where the post meets the clamp - to the bottom of the knurled nut. Take a note of the measurement. Leave the bike against the wall and climb on. Sit still in the normal riding position. Get a friend to measure again between the same two points. The difference should be around 10mm.

has to be set up so that it settles into place the correct amount under your weight. The post is supposed to give a little bit so that it's got room to spring upwards, supporting you if the bike drops into a dip. It has to be able to compress as well, so that if you hit a bump the bike can ride upwards, without kicking you upwards with it. The ideal is to set the preload on the spring inside the post, so that, when you sit on the bike, the natural resting point of the saddle is some way between the two extremes.

The total travel on seat posts isn't a great deal of distance, usually around 40mm (1½ in), so you're looking for the seat to sink about a quarter of that when you sit on it – about 10mm (3⁄8 in).

You'll need help for this bit as you have to sit on the bike and then let someone else measure how much difference you've made.

◀ **Step 2:** If the sag isn't right, undo and remove the clamp holding the seat post into the frame. Turn the post upside down. You'll be able to fit an Allen key in the cap in the bottom. If you've got more than 10mm sag turn the Allen key clockwise to add preload. If you've got less, turn the Allen key anticlockwise. It's important not to undo the cap so far it protrudes out of the end of the post.

◀ **Step 3:** You'll have to refit the post in the frame and repeat the measurements to check that the amount of sag is correct. It may take several goes to find the right place. Once you're confident about the sag, you'll need to reset your seat height.

Bar ends and grips

Bar ends (suitable for flat handlebars) went through a flourish of popularity some years ago when everybody owned a pair and everyone famous had a signature model. There are less about at the moment. I'm sure it's an aesthetic thing: they look a little odd on riser bars.

Bar ends are most useful for climbing because moving your weight forward over the front wheel helps keep it on the ground. They're great for short bursts of standing up on the pedals too – the angle is more comfortable, allowing your shoulders to open out so that you can get loads of air into your lungs. And it's nice to have a variety of hand positions when you're out on a long ride so that you don't get stiff and locked into a single position.

The profusion of shapes available can be confusing. Generally, choose short, stubby ones for climbing and longer, curved types for altering your riding position. I like ones with a machined pattern on the metal for extra grip.

The extra leverage that bar ends give you can be enough to twist your handlebars in their mounting – always check that your stem bolts are tight after fitting bar ends. Test that they will hold by standing in front of the bike with the front wheel between your knees. Push down hard on both bar ends. They shouldn't move on the bars, and neither should the bars move in the stem.

The end of your bar end, like handlebars, should always be finished off with a plastic plug. This protects you a little bit if you land on the end of your bar or bar end in a crash – an open end will make a neat round hole wherever it encounters parts of your body.

Just as vital for handlebar comfort are grips. There really are a lot of different choices here, so many that it's confusing rather than helpful. The most significant variable is grip thickness. Slim versions are lighter but less comfortable. Thick ones absorb more vibration, but this makes your bike feel less responsive – it's harder to feel what's going on if there's too much cushioning.

Your hand size also matters here. If you've got small hands, choose thinner grips. Dual density compounds, which have a softer, spongier layer over a firmer core, are a good compromise. Deep-cut patterns are better if your grips tend to get muddy and if you tend to ride when it's very hot, as smooth grips get slippery when you sweat onto them.

Grips that bolt on rather than stick on, like those made by Yeti, are a little more expensive but they are more secure and are easier to get on and off if you swap bars frequently. Each end of the grip has a locking aluminium collar that you tighten on with an Allen key.

Carbon bars need a little extra care – check whether your manufacturer recommends them, and follow any indicated torque settings carefully.

REFITTING BAR ENDS

◀ **Step 1:** Undo the bar-end fixing bolt (almost always a 5mm Allen key). Slide the bar ends off the bars. They usually come straight off easily, but if they don't, ease the clamp open by removing the fixing bolt completely and opening the gap with a screwdriver. This avoids scratching the bars.

◀ **Step 2:** Inspect the end of the bar and the bar end. Bar ends provide enough leverage for them to damage bars in a crash. If the end of the bar has been bent or dented, either replace the bar or choose not to refit the bar ends. Clean the interface and grease under the bolt head.

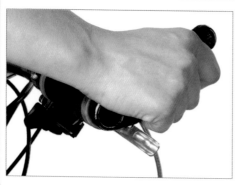

◀ **Step 3:** Refit the bar ends, tightening the bolt just enough to keep them in place. Sit on the bike and rotate the ends into a comfortable position. Check that both are pointing in the same direction, then tighten firmly. Stand in front of the bike and push down on the bar ends to check that they don't rotate on the bars and to see that the bars don't rotate under pressure.

Pedals and how to look after them

Clipless pedals are the standard for almost all speed-orientated bikes. They're also commonly known as SPD pedals, after the original Shimano version. (SPD stands for Shimano Pedalling Dynamics.) There are many versions available from different manufacturers. There isn't a standard-shaped cleat, so only use the cleats made by your pedal manufacturer – you can sometimes make others clip in, but you might not be able to clip out in a hurry.

Treat the threads of the pedals with grease or antiseize before fitting them. This treatment helps you to remove them and stops the cranks creaking as you pedal. Screw the pedals on firmly, or they will work loose and strip the threads, an expensive mistake to rectify. The thread that fixes the left-hand pedal is reversed, which means it screws on anticlockwise, and removes clockwise. This also means that the left-hand and right-hand pedals are not interchangeable.

This standard helps prevent the pedals from working loose and was originally adopted for fixed-wheel racing bicycles. Still in use today for track racing, these bikes have no ratcheting mechanism in the back wheel, so you can't freewheel. You brake by slowing down the pedalling. The reverse thread was vital. If the pedal bearings seized, the pedal, still being driven by the back wheel, would unwind from the cranks instead of snapping your ankle.

Pedals usually need more attention in the winter; seals are fine for summer but dirt works in as soon as it gets cold and muddy. Check by spinning the pedals on the axles. They should spin around at least twice with a good start. If not, it's time for a bearing service. Somehow, people neglect pedal bearings. I often come across otherwise well-cared-for bicycles with a pedal that almost needs a wrench to turn it. You might as well ride with the brakes dragging on the rim.

Often, one pedal continually needs more attention than the other. This is the side you fall off most, the side that gets stuck in the ground and picks up muck. Most mud falls off, but the rest is dragged in past the seals. Mud is not a good lubricant. I usually do both pedals in the same session, rather than just the sticky one. Once you have the tools out, doing both sides doesn't take much more effort than doing one.

Jet-washing destroys pedals faster than anything other than crashing. This is partly because people usually jet-wash from the side – the perfect angle to drive water and mud past seals that weren't designed to withstand pressure – and partly because the bindings accumulate mud so the pedals get extra spraying.

Pedals also suffer more than most other bearings. They get pushed as hard and are turned as often as bottom brackets, but in comparison their bearings are tiny and close together.

Choosing the right gear

Buying gear and accessories is one of the fun things about owning a bike but choose carefully. You'll find that some buys make a permanent place for themselves in your life, whereas other stuff, which once seemed like a good idea, is more trouble than it's worth.

Liquid

Cycling is hard enough work without being thirsty as well. A litre an hour is often thrown about as a guideline, but you should increase this in hot weather. Water bottles on your frame are a great low-tech solution, but protect the drinking nozzle if your trails take you through farms – muddy bottles don't bother me, but I don't like the thought of drinking farmyard debris.

Luggage

Most people carry everything on their backs or round their waists. I like to make an exception for tools, which I think are best carried in a seatpack under your saddle. They're usually oily, so you don't want them knocking around in your bag with clothes and sandwiches. And if you fall off, the last thing you want to land on is your toolbag.

For day rides, hydration systems with luggage capacity – as pioneered by CamelBak – are great. If you live somewhere wet make sure you get something waterproof – there is absolutely no point in carrying an extra layer all day then having to wring it out before you put it on. For hot climates concentrate on getting enough air circulating between bag and back to keep you as cool as possible. Larger bags take heavier loads, so look for wider breathable straps. Bags with lots of little pockets are more expensive, but it is worthwhile having different compartments if only so that you can keep your spare socks separate from your sandwiches.

Mudguards

If you live somewhere dry and dusty, skip this section. I do like cycling in all those places that don't have mud, and I agree it can be fun – especially because the weather is usually sunny – but I always worry that it's just not real. So, for real cyclists who get muddy, a word about mudguards.

I think that a front "crudguard", some variation on the theme of a piece of plastic strapped securely to your downtube (or equivalent), is an essential piece of gear. I have eaten too many pieces of tyre-grated cowpat in my life already and if not eating any more comes at the price of fixing an ugly piece of plastic to my bike, it's worth it. The guard also helps to stop bits of stuff from your front tyre getting flicked up into your eyes. Even if you wear glasses the angle of approach from the back of your tyre is perfect to slip lumps of crud under the bottom of your glasses. Strap on a front guard today.

If you can't bear to spend hard-earned cash on a plastic moulding, cut a water-bottle in half, punch some holes in it and ziptie it on. Guards can also make great emergency shovels and, with a good wash, make a lovely camping plate into the bargain.

Back mudguards aren't quite so useful, but if it's cold as well as wet, they make the leap into the essential items basket. I can't bear spray from my back wheel hitting the gap at the top of my jacket collar, trickling cold rain down my back. Again, I will put up with ugly plastic on my bike if it helps keep me warm and dry. And when I get home, I won't give up my place by the fire to a colder person with a prettier bike.

Lights

Night rides are fun. They bring on some kind of ancestral night vision that often let you ride sections faster at night because all the extraneous information your brain normally processes is invisible. I like it best when there's enough moon to see by – otherwise you'll need lights. The faster you go, the more powerful you need your lights to be – you need to be able to see far enough ahead to have time to react to things that appear in your pool of light before you arrive at them. And here's a safety message – don't do anything dangerous. If you can't see there, don't go there!

With lights under 5W in power, you have to move fairly slowly, even if there's a bit of moon. All batteries also contain a heap of environmentally unpleasant stuff and we use far too many of the disposable ones as it is, so treat yourself to at least 10W of rechargeable units. Make sure they're strapped on securely.

Fitting a rack

Follow the steps here to ensure your rack ends up flat, level and secure. Once this is done, you can either hang panniers off it or bungee your load to the top.

If your frame doesn't have the special lugs which are needed for bolting the rack to, you'll have to take your bike to the shop and investigate brackets.

As well as the p-clips mentioned on the opposite page, there is a whole range of specially made little gadgets for bolting the rack to the frame. The most common is a monostay adapter bracket, which allows you to bolt a rack onto the type of frame where the seat stays merge into one tube above the rear wheel. Rack-mounting seat collars can also save the day, especially on smaller frames. These replace the ring that you tighten to adjust your seat height, with a similar version that has additional threaded holes for the rack to bolt onto.

FITTING A RACK

▲**Step 1:** Work out which end is the front – more confusing than you think! The stays will bolt onto holes in the top of the rack. The holes on the back are for attaching reflectors and lights – in this picture, you can see a separate plate on the back. You may have to spread out the legs of the rack slightly to fit over the frame – the rack stays go on the outside of the frame on either side of the back wheel.

◀ **Step 2:** Bolt the legs of the rack to the outside of the frame, just above the back wheel axle. Use a washer under the head of each bolt. Take special care on the right-hand side of the bike as the bolt must not protrude through the frame, where it may interfere with the sprockets. If it does, either use a shorter bolt or take the bolt out and add extra washers directly under the bolt head. Don't tighten the bolts yet.

◀ **Step 3:** Next, attach the stays loosely to the front of the rack. Two common kinds consist of a pair of thin, flexible stays or a stiffer pair of stays with a selection of different-length extra sections to be bolted on. The stays bolt into slots rather than holes, so that you can adjust the position of the rack to suit the shape of your bike. If you're using shake-proof washers, you'll need a spanner to hold them while you tighten the bolts.

◀ **Step 4:** Next, fit the front of the stays loosely onto the frame. If you've got flexible stays, bend them gently so that you can get the bolts into the frame – take care not to cross-thread the bolts. If you've got a selection of joining pieces, choose a length that allows the stays to reach the frame.

◀ **Step 5:** With all the bolts loosely attached, you should now be able to pull the rack into place so that the top of the rack is level with the ground. Look from above too and check it's pointing straight forwards. You may have to twist it into place.

◀ **Step 6:** Once it's in place, go round systematically and tighten all the bolts – on the bottoms of the legs, on the stays and where the stays join to the frame. Check again that the bolts on the bottoms of the legs don't protrude through to the insides of the frame and interfere with your sprockets.

Fitting panniers

Once you've got your rack fitted, you're ready for panniers. These need to be attached securely since, if you pack them full of stuff and it starts shifting about while you ride, it makes your bicycle feel very unstable. The worst case scenario is your pannier partially bouncing off the rack and getting caught in your wheel... or bouncing somewhere into the distance when you go over a pothole. The chances are that you won't notice this happening...

Each pannier will have a pair of hooks that loop over the tubing of the rack. Better versions have a secondary clip that hooks under the tubing, so the pannier won't come off unless you release it. You'll generally find the rack is longer than the width between the pannier hooks, so you can choose how far back along the rack the pannier should sit. Keeping the weight as far forward as possible will maximise stability. However, if the panniers sit too close to you, you'll bang your heels on them every time you pedal – this is really irritating. You should be able to shift the position of the hooks sideways on the bag, choosing a position that prevents the bag shifting. As well as keeping your load stable, this helps to prevent the pannier hooks wearing through the rack tubing by constantly shuffling back and forth.

The bottom part of the bag must also be secured to the rack. This may seem superfluous when the bike is standing still, but out in the real world it's essential. If the back of the bike bounces around, the bottoms of the panniers flap outwards and may become dislodged.

Before you ride off, ensure that you've got any straps or bungees neatly tucked away. If they dangle down, they will inevitably flap about and get tangled in the back wheel, bringing you to an unexpected halt. If you're going to be carrying a lot of weight, just take a moment to check your rear-tyre pressure. A well-inflated tyre will give your wheel a bit of extra protection.

With panniers, it may seem tempting just to get one big one and stuff everything into it. But I would suggest two smaller ones rather than one big one. Although it's slightly more expensive, it's worth it for a couple of reasons. The first is that it's a lot easier to be organised if you've got two separate panniers – put your work papers in one side, and your sandwiches in the other. It's also less tiring to ride with an evenly loaded pair of bags than a single, heavy one. You rock from side to side as you pedal, so the bike dips slightly over to one side, and then down on the other. Evenly weighted bags will bob across like a pendulum, counterbalancing each other, whereas a single bag will have to be dragged back upright with every revolution of your feet.

POSITIONING A PANNIER

◀ **Step 1:** Pop the panniers on the rack and sit on the bike. Put your feet on the pedals with the ball of your foot directly over the pedal axle and pedal backwards. Move the pannier until your heel just clears the bag. Check your rear light is still visible. Push the backs of the bags in towards the wheel and check that they won't go far enough to get caught in the spokes.

◀ **Step 2:** Loosen the bolts that hold the pannier hook in place and slide the hooks so they trap the cross-struts of the rack or the rail across the back of the rack. This prevents the bag from sliding forwards and backwards on the rack. Retighten the hook bolts.

◀ **Step 3:** The bottom of the pannier needs to be attached to the rack stays, so that it can't flap outwards. In this case, a plastic tab must be positioned so that it hooks behind the rack leg. Other options include a strap or loop of elastic that hooks around the bottom of the pannier leg. The pannier may come with a hook to loop the strap around.

Glossary: the language of bikes

- **Aheadset:** The bearing that clamps the fork securely to the frame, while allowing the fork to rotate freely so you can steer. The now-standard Aheadset design works by clamping the stem directly to the steerer tube of the forks, allowing you to adjust the bearings by sliding the stem up and down the steerer tube with an Allen key.
- **Air spring:** Used in both suspension forks and shocks, an air spring consists of a sealed chamber pressurized with a pump. The chamber acts as a spring, resisting compression and springing back as soon as any compressing force is released. Air has a natural advantage as a spring medium for bicycles – it's very light.
- **Antiseize:** This compound is spread on the interface of two parts, preventing them sticking together. It is vital on titanium parts, since the metal is very reactive, and will seize happily and permanently on to anything to which it is bolted.
- **Axle:** The axle is the central supporting rod that passes through wheels and bottom brackets and around which they can rotate.
- **Balance screws:** These are found on V-brakes and cantilevers and allow you to alter the preload on the spring that pulls the brake away from the rim so that the two sides of the brake move evenly and touch the rim at the same time.
- **Bar ends:** Handlebar extensions that give you extra leverage when climbing and permit you to use a variety of hand positions for long days out.
- **Bottom bracket:** The main bearing connects the cranks through your frame. Often ignored because it's invisible, the smooth running of this part saves you valuable energy.
- **Brake arch:** On suspension forks, this is a brace between the two lower legs that passes over the tyre and increases the stiffness of the fork. It is called a brake arch even if your brakes are down by your hub.
- **Brake blocks:** These fit onto your V-brake or cantilever brakes. Pulling the brake cable forces them onto your rim, slowing you down.
- **Brake pads:** On disc brakes, these hard slim pads fit into the disc callipers and are pushed onto the rotors by pistons inside the brake calliper. They can be cable or hydraulically operated. Being made of very hard material, they last longer than you'd expect for their size, and, unlike V-brake blocks, do not slow you down if they rub slightly against the rotors. Contamination with brake fluid renders them useless instantly.
- **Brake pivot:** This is the stud on the frame or forks onto which cantilever or V-brakes bolt. Brakes rotate around the pivot so that the brake blocks hit the rim.
- **Cable:** This steel wire connects brake and gear levers to shifters and units. It must be kept clean and lubricated for smooth shifting and braking.
- **Calliper:** This mechanical or hydraulic disc brake unit sits over the rotor and houses the brake pads.
- **Cantilever:** (1) This older rim brake type connects to your brake cable by a second, V-shaped cable; (2) A suspension design that sees the back wheel connected to a swingarm that pivots around a single point. These designs are simple and elegant.
- **Casing:** Usually black, this flexible tube supports cables. Brake and gear casings are different: a brake cable has a close spiral winding for maximum strength when compressed; a gear casing has a long spiral winding for maximum signal accuracy.
- **Cassette:** This is the cluster of sprockets attached to your back wheel.
- **Chain-cleaning box:** This clever device makes chain cleaning less of a messy chore, increasing the chances of you doing it. (Now you just need a chain-cleaning, box-cleaning box.)
- **Chainring:** This is one of the rings of teeth your pedals are connected to.
- **Chainsuck:** A bad thing! When your chain doesn't drop neatly off the bottom of the chainring, but gets pulled up and around

the back, it jams between chainring and chainstay. Usually caused by worn parts, chainsuck is occasionally completely inexplicable.

◆ **Coil spring:** Usually steel but occasionally titanium, coil springs provide a durable, reliable conventional spring in forks and rear shocks.

◆ **Compression damping:** This is the control of the speed at which forks or shock can be compressed.

◆ **Crank:** Your pedals bolt onto cranks. The left-hand one has a reverse pedal thread.

◆ **Crank extractor:** This tool removes cranks from axles. There are two different kinds available – one for tapered axles, the other for splined axles.

◆ **Crankset:** The crankset is made up of three chainrings that pull the chain around them when you turn the pedals.

◆ **Cup-and-cone bearings:** These bearings roll around a cup on either side of the hub, trapped in place by a cone on either side. So that the wheel can turn freely with no side-to-side movement, set the distance between the cones by turning the cones so that they move along the axle threads.

◆ **Damping:** Damping controls how fast a suspension unit reacts to a force.

◆ **Derailleur hanger:** The rear derailleur bolts onto this part. This is usually the first casualty of a crash, bending when the rear derailleur hits the ground. Once bent it makes shifting sluggish. Luckily, hangers are quick and easy to replace, but there is no standard size; take your old one when you buy a new one, and get a spare for next time too.

◆ **Disc brake:** This braking system uses a calliper, mounted next to the front or rear hub, that brakes on a rotor or disc bolted to the hub. Hydraulic versions are very powerful. Using a separate braking surface also means the rim isn't worn out with the brake pads.

◆ **Dish:** Rims need to be adjusted to sit directly in the centreline of your frame, between the outer faces of the axle locknuts. Adding cassettes or discs to one side or other of the hub means the rim needs to be tensioned more on one side than the other to make

room for the extra parts.

◆ **Drivetrain:** This is a collective name for all the transmission components: chain, derailleurs, shifters, cassette and chainset.

◆ **End cap (cable end cap):** This is crushed onto the ends of cables to prevent them from fraying and stabbing you when you adjust them.

◆ **Ferrule:** This protective end cap for outer casing supports it where it fits into barrel-adjusters or cable stops.

◆ **Front derailleur:** This part moves the chain between the chainrings on your chainset.

◆ **Gear ratio:** Calculated by dividing chainring size by sprocket size and multiplying by wheel size in inches, the gear ratio determines the number of times your back wheel turns with one revolution of the pedal.

◆ **Hydraulic brakes:** Usually disc brakes, these use hydraulic fluid to push pistons inside the brake calliper against a rotor on the hub. Because brake fluid compresses little under pressure, all movement at the brake lever is accurately transmitted to the calliper.

◆ **Indexing:** The process of setting up the tension in gear cables so shifter click moves the chain across neatly to the next sprocket or chainring.

◆ **International Standard:** This term refers to both rotor fitting and calliper fitting. International Standard rotors and hubs have six bolts. International Standard callipers are fixed to the bike with bolts that point across the frame, not along it.

◆ **Lacing:** This technique is used to weave spokes to connect the hub to the rim. This part of wheelbuilding looks difficult, but it is easy once you know how.

◆ **Lower legs:** The lower parts of suspension forks, these attach to brake and wheel.

◆ **Modulation:** This is the ratio between brake lever movement and brake pad movement, or how your brake actually feels.

◆ **Nest:** This hanger or stop in a brake lever or gear shifter holds the nipple on the end of the brake or gear cable.

◆ **Nipple:** (1) This blob of metal at the end of a cable stops it slipping through the nest; (2) This nut on the end of a spoke secures it to the rim and allows you to adjust the spoke tension; (3) This perfectly ordinary part of a bicycle causes the pimply youth in the bike shop to blush furiously when asked for it by women.

◆ **Pinch puncture:** This happens when the tyre hits an edge hard enough to squash the tube on the tyre or rim and puncture it. It is also known as snakebite flat because it makes two neat vertical holes a rim's width apart. Apparently this is what a snake bite looks like, although I've never had a problem with snakes biting my inner tubes.

◆ **Pivot:** (1) This bearing on a suspension frame allows one part of the frame to move against another; (2) This is also a rod or a bearing around which part of a component rotates.

◆ **Preload:** This initial adjustment made to suspension springs to tune forks or shock to your weight is usually made by tweaking the preload adjustment knob, or by adding or removing air from air springs.

◆ **Rear derailleur:** This mechanism is attached to the frame on the right-hand side of the rear wheel. It moves the chain from one sprocket to the next, changing the gear ratio, when you move the shifter on your handlebars. It makes odd grinding noises when not adjusted properly.

◆ **Rebound damping:** Rebound damping controls the speed at which the fork or shock re-extends after being compressed.

◆ **Reverse thread:** The spiral of the thread runs the opposite way to normal: clockwise for undoing; counterclockwise for tightening.

◆ **Rotor:** Bolted to the hub, this is the braking surface of a disc brake.

◆ **Sag:** This is the amount of travel you use sitting normally on your bike. Setting up suspension with sag gives a reserve of travel above the neutral position.

◆ **Seal:** A seal prevents dirt, mud and dust from creeping into the parts of hubs, suspension units, headsets, bottom brackets and any other components where the preferred lubricant is grease rather than mud.

◆ **Socket:** Shaped like a cup, this spanner holds the bolt securely on all the flats.

◆ **Splines:** These ridges across a tool or component are designed to mesh with a matching part so that the two parts turn together.

◆ **Split link:** This chain link can be split and rejoined by hand without damaging the adjacent links.

◆ **Sprocket:** This toothed ring meshes with the chain to rotate the rear wheel. The cassette consists of a row of different-sized sprockets.

◆ **Stanchions:** This upper part of the suspension forks slides into the lower legs and contains all the suspension extras, including springs, damping rods and oil.

◆ **Standard tube:** For those who don't need tubelessness, this normal inner tube is designed to fit into a normal tyre.

◆ **Steerer tube:** This single tube extends from the top of the forks through the frame and has the stem bolted on the top.

◆ **Stiff link:** The plates of the chain are squashed too closely together to pass smoothly over the sprockets, and they jump across teeth rather than mesh with the valleys between teeth.

◆ **Travel:** Travel is the total amount of movement in the fork or shock. The longer the travel, the heavier and beefier the fork or shock must be.

◆ **Triggershifters:** This gear shifter features a pair of levers; one pulling, the other releasing, the cable.

◆ **Truing wheels:** The process of adjusting the tension in each spoke prevents the rim from wobbling from side to side when the wheel spins.

◆ **Tubeless:** In this weight-saving tyre design, the bead of the tyre locks into the rim, creating an airtight seal that needs no inner tube.

◆ **Twistshifters:** These gear shifters work by twisting the handlebar grip. Turning one way pulls through cable, while turning the other way releases cable.

◆ **UST:** Universal Standard for Tubeless. This is an agreed standard for the exact shape of rims and tyre beads. UST tyres and rims made by different manufacturers lock together neatly for an airtight seal.

◆ **V-brake:** In these rim brakes, two vertical (hence "V") units connected by the brake cable, hold the blocks.